THE
UFFIZI AND PITTI

FLORENCE

THE
UFFIZI AND PITTI
FLORENCE

BY

FILIPPO ROSSI

FORMER SOPRINTENDENTE OF
THE MUSEUMS AND GALLERIES OF
FLORENCE, AREZZO, AND PISTOIA

HARRY N. ABRAMS, INC. · PUBLISHERS
NEW YORK

CONTENTS

THE PLATES

Page 79

THE PICTURES IN MONOCHROME

Page 273

LIST OF ILLUSTRATIONS

Page 305

INDEX OF NAMES

Page 317

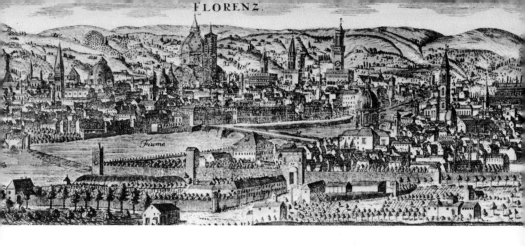

Foreword

Like other volumes in this series this book has a twofold purpose; to relate the history of a great gallery — in this case two great galleries in one city — and to illustrate some of the most important works concerned, with notes on their histories.

The Uffizi (' Offices ' : so called because the gallery forms part of a building erected by Vasari to house the offices of the State of Tuscany) and the Pitti (also known as the Galleria Palatina or Palatine Gallery, housed in the palace of the Grand Dukes) share a common history. In its still only partly realized ordering as a collection of works of art of every kind, the Uffizi Gallery dates from the sixteenth century. We owe its foundation to the enterprise of Grand Duke Francesco de' Medici, who decided to use the loggia crowning the palace that his father Cosimo I had built for the administrative and judicial departments of the Tuscan State. Thanks to Giorgio Vasari, this palace is among the most ingenious of all Renaissance solutions to problems of urban architecture.

To make room for the new building, demolition of the houses next to the church of San Piero Scheraggio had started as early as 1546, and the palace itself was begun in 1560. Five years later is was almost complete. A long, narrow *piazzale,* which extends towards the river, is faced by the central arch, which, though more majestic, is still in proportion with the two architraved porticos that lead to it, making up a whole of limpidly clear forms and perfectly balanced spaces. At the wish of Cosimo I, Vasari in 1564 began to link the new building with the Palazzo della Signoria and the Palazzo Pitti, which was acquired by Cosimo's wife Eleonora of Toledo in 1549, and had become the family residence. The connection with the Palazzo Pitti takes the form of a corridor from the top floor of the Uffizi, over a loggia bordering the river, across the Ponte Vecchio and along the backs of private houses until it finally reaches the Pitti.

The works of art that began to be arranged there in 1584 were not, however, just the fruit of one man's interest in collecting. On the contrary, they summarized an activity and enthusiasm that went back to the members of the Medici family, such as Giovanni di Bicci, who had founded its political and financial power. With their love of works of art, they were not only at the heart of the long humanist tradition begun in Florence in the fourteenth century, but they actively favoured and supported the movement of ideas and research which spread out from Florence through the whole of Italy in the fifteenth century, and which moulded one of the most fundamental and enduring aspects of modern European civilization.

In the course of the introduction it has naturally been necessary to allude to paintings that are now in other Florentine galleries, some of which (such as the Accademia) house parts of the grand-ducal collections, and some of which were founded in the nineteenth century, such as the Museo di San Marco, and the twentieth century (the Museo Andrea del Castagno). We have also mentioned the principal sculptures and works of applied art which have left the Uffizi at various times and are now in the Museo Archeologico, Museo Nazionale, and Museo degli Argenti in the Palazzo Pitti.

The note accompanying each colour plate, giving its history up to the day it entered the gallery, is based on all the archive material collected so far, and on the latest authoritative critical opinion.

The Origins of the Medici Family

GONFALONIER GIOVANNI DI BICCI DE' MEDICI

The name of Medici appears for the first time on the Florentine scene towards 1378. Originally from Mugello, this rich and active family had already provided the Florentine Republic with competent magistrates, bankers and merchants. Until the fifteenth century Florence was organized into 'guilds' of the major and minor arts, which included both professions and industries. In 1421 Giovanni di Bicci, who held the popular vote, was elected Gonfalonier. An apparently moderate man, he had behind him a powerful fortune, which enabled him, while depending on the support of the people, to make important loans to European princes and sovereigns.

Some of the earliest evidence of the Medici dealings with artists is provided by Vasari, who recounts that Giovanni di Bicci was represented, along with many other important contemporary Florentines, in Masaccio's Carmine fresco — unfortunately lost — showing the consecration of the church; also Zanobi Strozzi, who was a pupil of Fra Angelico, painted a portrait of him that in Vasari's day was in Duke Cosimo's repository. After the death of Giovanni in 1429, the Albizzi family, a powerful Florentine oligarchy, seem to have come to the fore.

A. BRONZINO. PORTRAIT OF GIOVANNI BICCI DE' MEDICI

COSIMO THE ELDER

Giovanni's son Cosimo, called the Elder, inherited his father's popularity, however, and despite his lack of official titles, proved himself a powerful adversary. Eventually, tired of finding him repeatedly blocking their way in business and politics, the leading Florentine families determined to get rid of him, and they bribed a gonfalonier to imprison, and then exile him in Padua, under false pretences. Nevertheless Cosimo remained the leader of the Florentine discontents, and in 1434, when the elections brought his supporters back to

A. BRONZINO. PORTRAIT OF COSIMO IL VECCHIO

power he returned to Florence in triumph. Carefully avoiding giving a tyrannical impression, and always calling upon the support of the people, he succeeded, by dint of hard work, determination and ambition, in becoming all-powerful.

Cosimo, even more than his father, was interested in all aspects of art, and his generosity towards artists can be seen not only in the buildings he raised at and outside Florence, but also in the works specially commissioned or acquired by him to adorn them, even though many of these works have unfortunately disappeared. Three paintings that he almost certainly commissioned from Paolo Uccello have survived from the decorations for one of the ground-floor rooms at the Palazzo Medici in the Via Larga. They represent *The Battle of San Romano,* which the Florentines won under the command of Niccolò da Tolentino on 1 June 1432 against the Sienese led by Filippo Maria Visconti, Duke of Milan. One of these three battle scenes is still in Florence at the Uffizi, but the others have found their way to the Louvre and the National Gallery, London. In the courtyard of the palace stood Donatello's bronze *David,* now at the Bargello, and in the garden at the back was the white marble *Marsyas tied to a Tree* that has been claimed, but with very little plausibility, to be the one now at the Uffizi, which traditionally was restored by Donatello. As no inventory of Cosimo's possessions has come down to us, it is impossible to establish which other works of art were in his palace, whether commissioned or merely acquired by him. Nevertheless, the Uffizi has Alesso Baldovinetti's altarpiece for the Villa Medici at Cafaggiolo, and Fra Filippo Lippi's for the Medici Chapel of the Noviciate in Santa Croce, with its Pesellino predella, both of which were commissioned by Cosimo the Elder. It also has the triptych by Nicolas Froment that Cosimo gave to the church of the Bosco ai Frati friary in the Mugello.

THE PALAZZO VECCHIO AND THE PIAZZA DELLA SIGNORIA

THE PALAZZO PITTI

In Cosimo's immediate entourage there was a rich merchant called Luca Pitti, one of the prince's most loyal supporters. Flattered by the favour in which he was held by the Medici, and by the role they allowed him to play, he commissioned Brunelleschi to build him a magnificent palace — the Palazzo Pitti — which he intended to be the counterpart of the Palazzo Medici on the opposite bank of the Arno. His ideas were too ambitious, however, and he was forced to leave the palace unfinished, having sunk most of his fortune in it (in 1549 it was bought by Eleonora of Toledo, wife of Cosimo I, and the grand-ducal court was installed there). After Cosimo the Elder's death Pitti tried vainly to establish himself with his successor.

PIERO THE GOUTY

When Cosimo died in 1464 Florence believed that she would now regain a certain degree of independence, but her hopes were short-lived, since Cosimo's eldest son, Piero, seized power immediately.

It was soon apparent that Piero, a weak character, was politically ineffectual, and he very quickly became unpopular. The political standing of the Medici was diminished during his term of government, although it was brief.

The Height of Power. Lorenzo the Magnificent

Piero the Gouty died in 1469, leaving two young sons, Lorenzo and Giuliano, around whom revolved a small court made up of artists and intellectuals, such as the pilosopher Marsilio Ficino, Verrocchio, and Botticelli. For some time the administration lay in the hands of supporters of the Medici, but Lorenzo soon began to aspire to power. His candidature was looked on askance by the leading Florentine families, and by various lesser nobles from the surrounding country, particularly by the Pazzi, who were the owners of a rival bank. They determined on the death of Lorenzo and Giuliano, and plotted the murder to take place during a service in the Cathedral. At the moment of the Elevation of the Host, an arranged signal, Giuliano collapsed, wounded to death, but Lorenzo, thanks to his friends, managed to escape. When the crowds realized what had happened, they flung themselves on the plotters, and an appalling scene of carnage took place; Lorenzo was borne aloft in triumph. He seized his chance. His first step was to take fierce reprisals which rid him of all his enemies, then, assuming almost royal powers, he managed to gain control of the whole government. In 1480 he effected a reconciliation with the Pope, and Florence, at peace with the Church, was at his feet.

THE DUOMO AND THE BAPTISTRY

So began this extraordinary reign, with its aura of brilliance which, despite the fact that there were various upheavals in Florence at that period, is more than merely legendary. The theories of the Humanists did not always coincide with the tendencies of contemporary art, and Savonarola's condemnations suggest that there was conflict at the heart of the Medici entourage, but it is thanks to Lorenzo that the theories were able to see the light, and survive to provoke the brilliant arguments whose effect on history will never be lost.

It is thanks to his patronage, which he made a central issue of his policy, that contemporary works of art offer such an illuminating account of every aspect of the civilization of the century. Lorenzo's concentration on enlarging the art collections of his ancestors was not simply inspired by a collector's enthusiasm, but by his own innate love of beautiful things, and by his need to seek out and frequent the greatest minds of his day. It is also thanks to him that painters and sculptors created masterpieces not only to decorate his own residences but also the churches and palaces of Florence and its outskirts. Goldsmiths, stone-workers, tapestry-workers, embroiderers, ivory-workers, all created in their various fields valuable works which point to the refined taste of the man who commissioned them, and above all to his ability to understand that the beauty of an object belonging to the so-called 'minor arts' is as worthy of attention as a painting or sculpture.

Following in the steps of his ancestors, he took a similar interest in architecture, In 1480 he commissioned Giuliano da Sangallo to build the Villa of Poggio a Caiano, and soon afterwards, in 1484, the church of Santa Maria delle Carceri in Prato — a town on the border of the Florentine state, on the way to Siena, which under Lorenzo's patronage was destined to become a second Pienza. His poetry is a reflection of his exceptional intelligence, and his political works complete the picture of this unique figure of the Quattrocento.

It is enough to study the inventory of his estate made at his death and published by Eugène Muntz (together with extracts from Piero's) to be convinced of his greatness. Here we find Uccello's three paintings of *The Battle of San Romano* referred to as being in the 'big ground-floor room known as Lorenzo's room'; they were accompanied over the *spalliera* and the couch by a picture of fighting dragons and lions, and a scene from the Legend of Paris, also the work of Uccello, and by a Pesellino hunting scene, all of which are now lost. In the same room there was a large tondo by Fra Angelico of the *Adoration of the Magi,* valued at 100 florins. Today it is thought that Fra Filippo Lippi also worked on it; it hangs in the National Gallery of Art, Washington. Lorenzo's room also contained three large canvases by Pollaiuolo showing the *Labours of Hercules,* of which an echo remains in the two little panels at the Uffizi.

In the antechamber of the adjoining room one saw the *SS. Jerome and Francis in the Wilderness* by Pesellino and Fra Filippo Lippi that is now in the Lindenau-Museum at Altenburg. There was also a Donatello bas-relief of Salome's dance, which is probably the one in the Musée Wicar at Lille. In the ' little room opposite the big room ' there was ' a scene in bronze over the fireplace with several horsemen, that is to say a battle ', which is none other than the Bertoldo di Giovanni bas-relief now in the Bargello. Elsewhere, above two doors, were the two busts of Piero and Giovanni di Cosimo by Mino da Fiesole, now also in the Bargello. In Giuliano's room there were

A. BRONZINO. PORTRAIT OF LORENZO THE MAGNIFICENT

more bronzes, such as ' the nude representing fear ', now ascribed to Pollaiuolo, ' a small scene in bronze measuring one *braccio* each way, in it a crucified Christ between two thieves with eight standing figures ', which is Bertoldo's *Cruxifixion,* and ' a Hercules crushing Antaeus, entirely of bronze ', which is the one by Pollaiuolo. Botticelli's *Pallas and the Centaur* is most likely identical with a painting described in the same inventory as being in Piero's room; and Rogier van der Weyden's *Entombment* is just as probably the ' altarpiece surrounded by a gilt frame, in which is painted the tomb of Our Lord unnailed from the cross and five other figures ', then in the chapel of the Villa Medici at Careggi.

This painting by Van der Weyden, and the one by Froment mentioned above, show what a lively interest the Medici were already taking in foreign art. The inventory contains references to works by other foreigners, such as Giovanni di Bruggia (Jan van Eyck) and Piero Cresti da Bruggia (Petrus Christus). These have probably been destroyed; certainly they can no longer be identified with any accuracy. Among non-Florentine artists, Squarcione is recorded, as the author of a tabernacle in Lorenzo's room, and of another work, *Judith with the head of Holofernes*. In this widening of their interest in art to include schools other than the Florentine, the Medici were undoubtedly helped by their own business organizations, which extended to many European countries. On various occasions their agents had dealings with the artists of the place where they were staying (one need only mention Tommaso Portinari, who sent the triptych by Hugo van der Goes to Florence); but it is not impossible that paintings such as Van der Weyden's were bought directly from the artist while he was visiting Italy. To these examples may be added Signorelli's painting of the Virgin, with several nudes in the background and two prophets in the corners of the imitation frame, which Vasari says was done for Lorenzo. The famous Libretto reliquary, which was given by Charles V of France to his brother Louis of Anjou, is mentioned as being in the office. It came into Piero de' Medici's possession, and afterwards passed to Lorenzo the Magnificent. Today it is in the Florentine Baptistry.

The inventory also includes references to many vessels in *pietra dura* or crystal. They are generally set, sometimes in silver-gilt, and often have gems in their foot or cover. But either because their setting has often been removed or altered, or because the actual indications of shape and material cannot always be interpreted with certainty, it is not easy to make out which of them are present among the numerous objects kept at the Palazzo Pitti. There is, however, one group there that does come from Lorenzo's collections. It comprises sixteen vessels with his name LAVR MED. engraved on their body, that are especially beautiful owing to their shape and sometimes also to their exquisite setting. Another six still remain in the treasury of San Lorenzo : they were turned into reliquaries at the direction of Clement VII, who gave them to the basilica. This is a truly remarkable array of vessels in *pietra dura,* some perhaps going back to classical antiquity and some possibly produced by Oriental workshops, but also by Italian, and above all, Venetian ones. Their elegant forms combine with the rare and precious materials to achieve an exceptionally beautiful effect. Another aspect of Lorenzo's taste is revealed in the great many cameos and intaglios, mostly set in rings or mounted in gold. Their number was continually being increased by the antique examples that Lorenzo bought, and also by ones from the hands of the contemporary craftsmen he patronized, almost bringing about a renaissance of this once so prolific art. Some of these antique gems bearing Lorenzo's name are now in the Museo Archeologico in Florence, and some of the fifteenth-century ones are in the Pitti. But most of them are in the Museo Nazionale at Naples, having passed through the Farnese collection and various French and English collections.

Some of the antique sculptures owned by Lorenzo, which were probably in the garden of San Marco, have been identified through other sources : the bronze head of a horse, perhaps fifth-century Greek work, now at the Museo Archeologico; and the so-called head of Scipio, a gift from Niccolò Valori, that of Agrippa, a gift from Sixtus IV, and the sleeping Cupid, a gift from Giuliano da Sangallo, now at the Uffizi. All these identifications are, however, doubtful, or at any rate not supported by reliable evidence. Moreover, it is not impossible that other antique sculptures that once belonged to Lorenzo, but then passed into other hands are present in the Florentine collections. But such movements and the restorations that may have been carried out make further identifications difficult.

Two of the Uffizi's most famous works, the *Primavera* and *Birth of Venus* by Botticelli, come from a member of the collateral branch started by Cosimo the Elder's brother Lorenzo. So does Lorenzo di Credi's *Venus,* all three having been painted for Lorenzo di Pierfrancesco, who became the owner of the villa at Castello near Florence. But as the land for the villa was bought during Lorenzo's minority, and as one of his guardians was Lorenzo the Magnificent, the latter could have had more to do with the commissioning of these masterpieces than might appear.

CAFAGGIOLO. A MEDICI VILLA

The last years of Lorenzo the Magnificent's life were unfortunately blighted by illness, and by the upheavals caused by the fanatical monk Savonarola. In 1490 Lorenzo retired to his villa at Careggi, where he died in 1492. He was buried without pomp, and his bier was followed by silent crowds mourning for the man whom they had called the 'Father' of Florence.

21

COURTYARD OF THE PALAZZO DEL PODESTÀ, NOW THE MUSEO NAZIONALE

Troubled Years. Greatness and Decadence

Lorenzo's eldest son Piero, who succeeded him, benefited at first from the popularity of his father, but his ruthless and precipitate nature quickly made him unpopular. When Charles VIII of France invaded Italy in 1494 Piero proved unable to defend either his own dignity or his possessions, and with no attempt at resistance, he left everything to the mercy of his enemies within and without. The result was that the populace, together with the French, set about plundering the Medici homes, while the Signoria stepped in to confiscate much of what remained. Only a part of the gold and silver objects were entrusted in time by the Medici themselves to people who succeeded in preserving them from further disasters. We do not know which and how many things escaped the pillage or the confiscation and which of them remained in Piero's possession. A lot of the confiscated objects were sold by auction, but many others met a different fate, such as Donatello's *Judith,* which was set up in front of the Palazzo della Signoria; or the library, which, given as a pledge and then sold to the friars of San Marco, was redeemed some years later by Cardinal Giovanni, the future Leo X. This applies to the silverware, bronzes and statues, whose vicissitudes are indicated in a few documents, but no information has come down to us about what happened to the many paintings mentioned in Lorenzo's inventory, apart from a brief note in the diary of Luca Landucci on the auction-sale, which included paintings, that took place during August 1495, in Orsanmichele. Piero made one unsuccessful attempt to re-enter Florence in 1497, and in 1503 he died at the battle on the Garigliano in which Gonzalo de Córdoba defeated the French.

GIOVANNI, GIULIO, GIULIANO II, LORENZO II, IPPOLITO AND ALESSANDRO. LORENZACCIO'S CRIME

A troubled time lay ahead for Italy, and particularly for Florence. During the wars with France, and then with Spain, the gonfalonier Pier Soderini briefly replaced the Medici as head of the city. He in turn was forced to flee when Lorenzo the Magnificent's second son, Cardinal Giovanni, entered Florence victoriously at the head of his condottieri and the numerous troops in his pay. He did not remain for long, however, as he was elected Pope Leo X. Giovanni handed the succession as leader of Florence to Giulio de' Medici, the posthumous illegitimate son of Giuliano (who had been assassinated earlier in the famous *coup*). But Giulio, who preferred his Rome residence, hardly ever lived in Florence, and the authority fell on Giuliano II, the third son of Lorenzo the Magnificent. When he died in 1516, he was succeeded by his nephew, Lorenzo II, the eldest son of Piero II and grandson of Lorenzo the Magnificent.

Lorenzo II assumed complete authority and succeeded in making peace with the King of France, sealing the settlement by his marriage to a Frenchwoman, Madeleine de la Tour d'Auvergne (Catherine de' Medici was to be her daughter). He died soon after, however, and Giulio returned for a while to Florence, until he was elected Pope Clement VII two years later, whereupon he appointed two members of his family close to his heart to take his place. Ippolito and Alessandro were both illegitimate sons, Ippolito of Lorenzo II and Alessandro of Giuliano II. The Florentines agitated, war with Spain broke out again, and the two princes were forced into exile. But in 1532 Alessandro was recalled, and given the title of Duke of Tuscany, thanks to the support of Charles V, with whom he had effected a reconciliation and whose daughter, Margaret of Austria, he married. His violence and abuse of power provoked constant plots around him; one of them has been immortalized by Musset. Alessandro had befriended Pier Francesco de Lorenzo de' Medici (a descendant of the younger branch of the family of Lorenzo, brother of Cosimo the Elder), named Lorenzino, later Lorenzaccio, on account of his small stature. Lorenzaccio's character was strange and extreme. He had at one time planned to kill Pope Clement VII, his relative; then, when he had been hounded from Rome for mutilating the bas-reliefs of the Arch of Constantine, he took refuge in Florence, where he became one of Alessandro's favourite companions. But Alessandro so irritated him with his tyrannical and violent behaviour that in 1527 Lorenzaccio, already unbalanced, assassinated him. Then, without thinking of taking advantage of his crime, he fled in panic to Bologna, Constantinople, Paris, and finally Venice, where he was murdered himself.

TAZZA FARNESE, ALEXANDRIAN CAMEO

This stormy period was naturally unpropitious for the progress of art, and the Medici collections suffered. While the court was torn by conflicting passions and the Medici were on the Florentine throne there was little time to spare for the task of preserving and adding to Lorenzo the Magnificent's legacy. The Medici palaces were overthrown, the collections repeatedly dispersed, and there was no chance of reviving the splendour which had made the family famous in the fifteenth century. After Alessandro's death, all that remained in the possession of his widow Margaret of Austria eventually ended up, through her remarriage in 1538 to Ottavio Farnese, in the Farnese collections (now at the Museo Nazionale in Naples). Besides the gems at Naples engraved with Lorenzo the Magnificent's name, already mentioned, Margaret's belongings included what later became known as the Tazza Farnese. This is a big Alexandrian cameo in grey onyx on a brown ground, bearing on the outside a gorgon's head and on the inside an allegorical glorification of the Nile. It belonged first to Pope Paul II and them from 1471 to Lorenzo the Magnificent. In Lorenzo's inventory it is valued at 10,000 florins — more than any other object there.

The Age of the Grand Dukes

COSIMO I, DUKE OF FLORENCE AND GRAND DUKE OF TUSCANY.
THE BUILDING OF THE UFFIZI AND ACQUISITION OF THE PALAZZO PITTI

With Alessandro the elder branch of the Medici family came to an end. His successor was Cosimo I, and to understand his place in the Medici family tree it is necessary to look backwards in time. In 1496 or 1497 Giovanni, the son of Pier Francesco, cousin of Piero the Gouty, had married Catherine Sforza, the widow of Girolamo Riario. Their son Giovanni delle Bande Nere was to be the father of Cosimo I, who succeeded Alessandro in Tuscany.

With the support of Charles V, and by dint of his own political ability, Cosimo established the Tuscan state on a sound basis; he might well be called its founder. Towards the end of his reign Pope Pius V awarded him the title of Grand Duke, and soon afterwards he was crowned in Rome. His reign introduced a prosperous and peaceful period for the world of arts and letters, which he patronized. He reassembled what was left of the Medici collections and set about adding to them. Vasari tells us that in his time the majority of the recovered objects were preserved in Duke Cosimo's *guardaroba*, or repository, at the Palazzo della Signoria, which as early as 1540 had become the sovereigns' residence. There is an inventory from 1553 ' of the repository and the things that are in the palace of His Most

Illustrious Excellency ', and it shows that by continually making new acquisitions Cosimo had succeeded in creating another hoard of treasure. This was to become the main nucleus of the famous Medici repository, which foreigners never failed to visit, and from which objects of every kind were often transferred to the gallery, or to the other palaces and the many grand-ducal villas, in accordance with the tastes and whims of the ruler. The fairly detailed descriptions in the inventory make it possible to identify many of the works of art that afterwards went to make up the gallery.

In one of the rooms of the Duke's living quarters the presence is mentioned of a Pontormo *Virgin* that could be the one with the infant St John at the Uffizi. Another room in the same part of the palace contained a *Bacchus* by Bandinelli (perhaps the *Adam* begun for the Cathedral but turned into a *Bacchus* and given to the Duke, which is now at the Pitti), Sansovino's *Bacchus,* and an unfinished *David* by Michelangelo (now both in the Bargello). Raphael's painting in the same room showing *Leo X with Two Cardinals* is, however, the work from the Pitti which is now at the Uffizi; and there was also the *Venus and Cupid* by Pontormo after a Michelangelo cartoon. In other surroundings could be seen a ' likeness of the Dwarf Morgante on canvas front and back view' which is the one by Bronzino still in the reference section of the Uffizi, and many other portraits that cannot be securely identified, not to mention the statue of *Minerva* found at Arezzo and now among the bronzes at the Museo Archeologico.

In the repository proper, which was furnished by Cosimo with big cupboards of carved walnut which Ignazio Danti adorned on the outside of the doors with Ptolemy's geographical maps, we find a 'portrait on canvas of cardinal Ippolito de' Medici dressed in the Hungarian style ', which is the one by Titian at the Pitti; the panel portrait of the Duke of Milan and Bertoldo's *Battle,* both previously recorded in Lorenzo's inventory; and 'the portrait of the Duchess and of Don Francesco from Bronzino's hand', which is now in the Tribuna of the Uffizi. Then, in the private repository, we find Titian's *Portrait of Aretino,* which is today at the Pitti; portraits of *SS. Cosmas and John the Baptist* by Bronzino that may have been those intended for Duchess Eleonora's chapel at the Palazzo della Signoria; the three portraits, also by Bronzino, of Cosimo's children, Maria, Francesco (who may actually be Ferdinando), and Garsia, which again are perhaps those now in the Tribuna of the Uffizi; Bandinelli's bronze heads of Cosimo and Eleonora, now at the Bargello, and an oval relief with another likeness of Cosimo, also at the Bargello.

There were plenty of tapestries; those with the Months, on cartoons by Bacchiacca, now at the Uffizi; the Flemish ones with scenes from the story of Adam, that are at the Accademia; and a number of those woven at the Florentine factory that today are scattered in various important buildings. Many of the antique and recent bronzes listed in this inventory are likewise now at the Museo Archeologico, or the Bargello, such as the ' nude representing fear' previously recorded in Lorenzo's inventory, a *Venus,* a *Cleopatra,* a *Leda,* another *Venus,* and a *Hercules* by Bandinelli; Michelangelo's torso of a river god, and Cellini's relief of a dog; Sansovino's *Laocoön* and the Hercules seal. Also in the repository were the miniatures of the Medici family commissioned by Cosimo I from Bronzino and referred to by Vasari in his life of the artist.

Cosimo's love of antiquity led him to secure bronzes such as the *Chimera* found at Arezzo, or the so-called *Orator,* that came from Umbria, as well as the *Minerva* already mentioned. Each fresh discovery of ancient coins and inscriptions saw the Duke among the most eager purchasers; and he was no less interested in culture generally, as is shown by his founding of an academy of fine arts and of drawing, and by his action in commissioning Cristofano dell' Altissimo to copy the series of portraits of sovereigns and famous men that Paolo Giovio had assembled in the museum at his delightful villa on Lake Como. Cosimo had the series continued, thus starting a collection that is now of great iconographic value, both because Giovio's originals have nearly all been destroyed, and because some of those added by Cosimo or his successors have considerable importance as unique evidence of how a personage looked.

As early as 1531 the surviving statues Lorenzo had brought together in the garden of San Marco were joined at the Palazzo Medici by the copy of the *Laocoön* that had been made by Baccio Bandinelli for Francis I of France and then sent by Clement VII to Florence.

THE PORTICO OF THE UFFIZI

Cosimo I also added many others, such as the Farnese-type *Hercules* now in the courtyard of the Palazzo Pitti, the two groups of *Menelaus* and *Patroclus* at the Pitti and in the Loggia della Signoria, and the torso restored by Cellini as a Ganymede, now at the Bargello.

In 1564 Cosimo I handed over the management·of public affairs to his eldest son Francesco, who received the title of Prince Regent. He continued, nevertheless, to busy himself with the works that were proceeding briskly above all in the Palazzo della Signoria, which came to be called the Palazzo Vecchio after the head of state had gone to live in the Palazzo Pitti. Cosimo, as we have seen, had in fact bought the Palazzo Pitti for Eleonora of Toledo to replace the austere and uncomfortable Palazzo della Signoria. The installation of the court in the new building involved a host of designers, sculptors, painters and architects (especially Bartołommeo Ammannati). At the same time, on the other bank of the Arno, Vasari was building the Uffizi. Possibly Cosimo himself had the idea that the big upper loggia of the new building, intended to accommodate the many governmental departments of the dukedom, was the right place for setting out most of the vast number of sculptures, old and new, that now crowded the family's palaces, villas and gardens. But he did not begin to realize the scheme, partly, perhaps, because of his declining health.

FRANCESCO I AND THE CREATION OF AN ART GALLERY IN THE UFFIZI

When Cosimo died in 1574 he was succeeded by Francesco I as the second Grand Duke of Tuscany. (His title had been confirmed by the Emperor Maximilian II.) Francesco was debauched and cruel, and his violent methods made him very unpopular. He was married to Jeanne of Austria with whom he had several children — including Maria de' Medici who was to marry Henri IV and become Queen of France, but he had fallen violently in love with Bianca Capello, a member of the Venetian nobility, who became his mistress and whom he married on the death of Jeanne. He died himself in 1587. His greatest merit was to enlarge the Medici art collections, and to commission Bernardo Buontalenti, one of the best architects of the period, to adapt the loggia of the Uffizi to carry out his father Cosimo's ideas.

It was the east corridor — the one nearest the Palazzo della Signoria, which had already been connected with the Uffizi — that received the nucleus of what was called the Statue Gallery, thus introducing for the first time the word 'gallery' in the sense of a collection of works of art methodically displayed and in harmony with its surroundings. The ceiling of the corridor was decorated with grotesques in the manner of those Raphael did for the Vatican loggias, and the work was carried out by three Florentine late-Mannerist painters : Giovan Maria Butteri (c. 1540-1606), a pupil of Bronzino and assistant of Alessandro Allori; Giovanni Bizzelli (c. 1556-1607), a pupil of Allori; and Alessandro Pieroni (c. 1550-1607), another pupil of Bronzino and, as an architect, of Buontalenti. Buontalenti himself had the task of building the Tribuna, which, thus named from the start, was decorated by Bernardino Poccetti and covered by a dome lined with mother-of-pearl; he also adapted some neighbouring rooms for the same purpose.

When the many sculptures had been placed in the corridor (and this must have happened after 1581, the date recorded in one of the

A. BRONZINO. PORTRAIT OF BIANCA CAPELLO

compartments of the ceiling adorned with grotesques), the portraits copied from those in Paolo Giovio's collection were displayed on the upper part of the inner wall. In the eight corners of the Tribuna marble statues were disposed, including a sleeping Cupid in basanite. All around on the ebony shelves there were statuettes and the most varied objects, which stood out against the walls covered with red velvet : from pictures to bronzes, miniatures to enamels, ivories to jewels. They surrounded a cabinet of exceptional value made of rare woods, adorned by gems and a series of small imperial busts in precious stones and bas-reliefs in gold referring to Francesco's principal achievements. A few of these, now in the Silver Museum at the Pitti, are the only witnesses to the splendour that was not enough to save the cabinet from destruction. Culminating in a small, gem-encrusted dome that corresponded symmetrically to the Tribuna's, and bore a lantern topped by a crystal ball, it contained what was then the richest collection of coins, medals, cameos and intaglios.

The inventory, recording as early as 1589 the contents of the Tribuna, shows the Medici collection to have been so large that is seems impossible that it could all have been contained there. Among the paintings were works by Andrea del Sarto (the portrait of a young woman with a volume of Petrarch's Sonnets, then ascribed to Pontormo, and the *St John the Baptist* now at the Pitti), Fra Bartolommeo (the small tabernacle with the *Circumcision, Nativity* and *Annunciation*), Piero di Cosimo *(Perseus freeing Andromeda),* Francesco Granacci and Andrea del Sarto (the panels for the nuptial chamber of Pier Francesco Borgherini and Margherita Acciaiuoli), Domenico Beccafumi (the *Holy Family* tondo now at the Pitti), and at least six paintings by Raphael : *St John the Baptist in the Wilderness, Portrait of Leo X with Two Cardinals, Madonna del Cardellino, Madona dell'Impannata, Madonna della Seggiola,* and *Vision of Ezekiel.* These were accompanied

THE TRIBUNA

by Pontormo's *Virgin and Child with the Infant St John* and *Leda and the Swan* (the latter then attributed to Andrea del Sarto), Alessandro Allori's *Hercules and the Muses* and *Abraham sacrificing Isaac,* Sodoma's *Capture of Christ,* the so-called *Fornarina* then thought to be by Raphael but now by Sebastiano del Piombo, and Gerard David's *Deposition,* then attributed to Lucas van Leyden. Besides these works still present in the galleries, the Tribuna contained many others that either no longer form part of the Florentine collections (such as Raphael's *Madonna Canigiani,* which went to Germany with the dowry of the last of the Medici when she married the Elector Palatine), or that cannot now be reliably identified. Naturally there was a predominance of Florentine or Tuscan artists and ones who, like Raphael, had had lasting ties with Florence; but it is interesting to note how they were joined by Federigo Fiammingo (Friedrich Sustris), by Civetta (Herri met de Bles of the famous *Copper Mines*), and, through several paintings, by Giorgione and Parmigianino. It is a sign that the ruler's taste, and that of his predecessors, still had the breadth shown by the fifteenth-century Medici. Very soon the painting of the other regions of Italy and Europe would be represented even more fully, helped by the confluence in the Medici collection of big legacies that, as we shall see, effectively combined to increase its importance, partly owing to the varied personalities of the original owners.

There were a great many antique marble sculptures in the Tribuna, as well as ancient and modern bronzes. The latter included numerous works by Giambologna, among them the silver *Labours of Hercules.* Beside the many miniatures and ivories, the objects in *pietra dura* and rock-crystal were numerically predominant, reflecting one of Grand Duke Francesco's chief partialities. Some of the most important examples can still be admired in the Silver Museum at the Palazzo Pitti, such as the turquoise head of a Roman emperor (then thought to be Julius Caesar but now identified as Tiberius); the lapis-lazuli vessel, designed by Buontalenti, with Francesco's initials and the date 1583; the rock-crystal vessel shaped like a galley, from the workshop of the Saracchi, who worked for the Grand Duke; the one of jasper in the form of Hercules overcoming the Hydra, probably by a Tuscan artist; and the big cameo by Giovanni Antonio de' Rossi showing Cosimo I with his family.

During the same years the rooms next to the Tribuna must have been arranged and decorated. On the ceiling of one can be seen astronomical apparatus, and it must have contained the mathematical instruments. Of those that follow the Tribuna, the first has seventeenth-century decorations and the ceiling of the second shows entertainments in the courtyard of the Palazzo Pitti and the piazze of the Signoria, Santa Croce, and Santa Maria Novella, while the other three have scenes of military actions or workshops for producing arms and armour. From the start these rooms held the Medici armoury, which comprised examples of historic and artistic value, including some oriental pieces and apparently a few from America as well. In the following centuries this armoury became quite remarkably substantial, but unfortunately not many pieces remain, owing to a sale at the end of the eighteenth century.

Francesco's passion for the most ingenious operations, such as melting rock-crystal, manufacturing porcelain, or executing works in *pietra dura,* sometimes led him to carry out the processes himself; Bocchi mentions in his *Bellezze di Firenze* (published in 1591) that the Tribuna contained a 'rich-looking and wonderful mound of pearls and jewels constructed by the hand of Grand Duke Francesco'. No doubt he was able to indulge his passion more often when, wishing to have Buontalenti rebuild the Casino di San Marco, he moved all his craftsmen, who had previously worked at the Casino, to the gallery.

In the course of his reign Francesco did not fail to enlarge his collections, above all with marble statues, medals, engraved stones, and other ancient works of art that he continually bought or received as gifts, making use of antiquarians and the goodwill of other Florentine collectors such as Niccolò Gaddi. But the person who chiefly helped him was his brother Ferdinando, a cardinal in Rome and later his successor. It appears to have been Ferdinando who sent him Michelangelo's *Bacchus,* which was in the gallery by 1591, and also the sarcophagus with the fall of Phaethon.

FERDINANDO I

When he mounted the throne in 1587 Ferdinando must have transferred to Florence much of what he had collected in Rome in the villa on the Pincio acquired from Cardinal Ricci, as well as continuing the work on the gallery by adding new rooms. His taste and his passion for antiquity are attested by his purchases, which include the Medici *Venus*, the group representing the myth of Niobe, the *Wrestlers*, the *Apollo*, and the Capranica marbles. All these were only moved to Florence at a later date. During his reign what is still known as the Map Room was prepared, where the Jesuit Serrati painted maps showing the territories of the Grand Duke of Tuscany. The collection of astronomical instruments and apparatus was enlarged and joined by natural-history specimens, though Ferdinando himself transferred the latter to the museum of Pisa Academy in 1595. At this period the gallery also had attached to it a 'foundry', or pharmaceutical laboratory, whose products were extolled by those who visited it. Ferdinando's zeal in obtaining pictures and rarities of every kind never flagged during the twenty odd years of his reign. His name is also connected with the acquisition of the famous diamond called the Florentine, which was then valued at over two and a half million francs.

The appearance of the gallery round about 1600 is described in the notes on a canzone written by G.B. Elicona for the marriage of Marie de' Medici to Henri IV of France, which took place that year. These notes are the work of the Italian traveller Filippo Pigafetta, who was in Ferdinando I's service between 1592 and 1603. In the east corridor or gallery, 'so-called using the French word', arranged at the sides on the tiled floor he saw antique marble statues, 'human and of stone' (actually the Wild Boar and the two Hellenistic Molossian Hounds were already there), as well as modern ones by Michelangelo and others. On the walls were the portraits of the Medici and the copies from Giovio's collection. The Tribuna and the neighbouring rooms are thus described : ' ...built as a rotunda, roofed in lead by an elegant and graceful dome, and adorned with a variety of precious things, ancient and modern, all covered in red and impearled, with gold, silver, and silk, like a heavenly abode, a starry retreat... Almost its equal is the other chamber, in which Her Serene Highness the Grand Duchess [Christine of Lorraine] greatly enjoys collecting together such a mass of valuable and splendorous products of nature and art. Next to it the rooms begin, including those of the arms, in which ancient means of attack and defence from every nation are assembled,

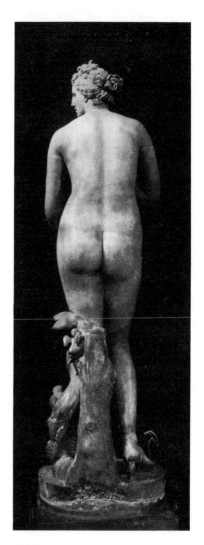

THE MEDICI VENUS

together with most exquisite modern examples, and even some from
the New World and India, as well as extremely delicate workshops
for making arquebuses and other arms and implements... With these

37

is connected the room in which the mathematical instruments are kept... Above the Offices on the right [west] side are located the rooms for the various crafts of the goldsmiths, the horologists, the carvers of rock-crystal, who make the stones and different jewels shiny and smooth, and those who fit together their parts in tables as multicoloured inlays and make mosaics... And first of all at the end of that gallery over the vault of the loggia there extends the garden planted with trees that are always in leaf and with flowers... Nearby is the foundry... where most expert masters distil waters of scented flowers and herbs, and oils for druggists and apothecaries... and electuaries [that the sovereigns present] to prelates, ambassadors, and gentlemen, and to everyone, benevolently, as fast-acting remedies'.

COSIMO II

Ferdinando died in 1608, leaving the throne to his son Cosimo II, who had a short, unhappy reign, owing to the early age at which he succeeded and to his poor health, especially in his latter years. Under him the decoration of the Tribuna was completed, as is shown by his name and the date 1610 in an angle of the dome. It was during his reign that a painting by Correggio, the *Virgin adoring the Child,* came as a gift from the Duke of Mantua, Ferdinando Gonzaga. Cardinal Anton Maria del Monte presented him with Caravaggio's *Medusa,* while Thomas Howard, Earl of Arundel, gave him the *Portrait of Sir Richard Southwell* by Hans Holbein the Younger. From this time dates the valuable relief in *pietra dura,* gold, and cut diamonds showing the Duke in prayer. Intended for a frontal he wanted to give to an altar in Milan Cathedral, it was executed in 1619 by Orazio Mochi on a design by Giovanni Bilivert, and is now in the Pitti.

FERDINANDO II, THE URBINO INHERITANCE, THE COLLECTIONS OF CARDINALS CARLO AND GIOVANCARLO, AND OF PRINCE MATTIA. THE ENLARGEMENT OF THE UFFIZI AND FIRST STEPS TOWARDS A MUSEUM IN THE PALAZZO PITTI

Cosimo's son Ferdinando II, who mounted the throne in 1620, devoted much attention to the gallery during the fifty years of his reign.

He gave his brother Leopoldo (later a cardinal) the task of planning the decoration for the ceilings of the other two corridors, to which the gallery was now being extended. This Leopoldo did in consultation with his librarian Ferdinando del Maestro, Canon Lorenzo Pantiatichi, and Alessandro Segni. It was agreed that each of the main sections of the west corridor should be devoted to an art or branch of learning, where the portraits of Florentines who had gained most distinction in that particular field should hang. Alternating with those scenes, in the minor compartments there were to be representations of the exploits of the cities belonging to the Tuscan state, and of their inhabitants' most glorious deeds. In the south corridor, on the other hand, would be illustrated the virtues of the Grand Dukes from Cosimo I to Cosimo II, the Council of Florence (1439), the Florentine saints, the founding of the Order of St Stephen, and SS. Dominic, Francis, Charles Borromeo, and Filippo Neri. The work, which began in 1658, was undertaken by some of the best-known painters of the times, such as Cosimo Ulivelli and Jacopo Chiavistelli, as well as by lesser men, such as Chiavistelli's pupils Angiolò Gori, Giuseppe Masini, Giuseppe Tonelli, Giovanni Sacconi, and Rinaldo Botti.

Ferdinando II made an extremely important addition to the gallery through purchases of antique sculptures. In 1669 he brought the *Hermaphrodite* for 2,000 scudi from the Ludovisi family, together with thirteen heads, including the very valuable one of *Cicero,* and a small bronze *Jupiter.* In 1657 he acquired from Bologna a Hellenistic statue of *Venus,* as well as other pieces of sculpture. Then shortly after 1666 he obtained the Hellenistic group of *Cupid and Psyche,* closely followed by the Christian oil-lamp with SS. Peter and Paul, a notable array of inscriptions from Africa, and probably also the *Dionysus leaning on a Satyr,* which is also Hellenistic.

But the greatest increment to the Medici collections during Ferdinando II's reign came through the legacy his wife Vittoria della Rovere received when the Della Rovere line became extinct in 1631 at the death of Duke Francesco Maria II. This inheritance embraced the famous *Idolino* from Pesaro, discovered in 1530, and an extremely rich armoury, which went to join that of the Medici, and shared the same sad fate. Among the many other precious things there was a collection of Urbino majolica and numerous paintings by artists of renown.

These included the *Portrait of Federico di Montefeltro* and of his wife *Battista Sforza* by Piero della Francesca; Raphael's *Self-Portrait,* and likenesses of *Julius II* and *Cardinal Bernardo Dovizi da Bibbiena ;* Bronzino's Portrait of *Guidobaldo II della Rovere ;* a really outstanding group of Titians comprising the *Portrait of Francesco Maria I della Rovere* and of his wife *Eleonora Gonzaga,* the portrait known as *La Bella,* that of a nobleman once thought to be English, the *Venus of Urbino,* the *St Mary Magdalen,* and, as a school work, the *Portrait of Sixtus IV ;* a Palma Vecchio *Judith ;* Sebastiano del Piombo's *Martyrdom of St Agatha ;* and Baroccio's *Portrait of Francesco Maria II* and of *Federico of Urbino.* Along with these exceptionally important paintings, many others came from Urbino that, though of merit, do not have the same interest. Some of those mentioned in the lists made at that time cannot now be identified, while others subsequently left the collection in various circumstances. To that of Florence had thus been added another no less famous princely collection, the fruit of an equally longstanding tradition of patronage. It was a collection that was well fitted to integrate and complement that of the Medici, in its absence of classical sculptures and medals, in which the Medici collection abounded, and the preponderance of non-Tuscan pictures, which the Medici had not until then had occasion to acquire.

A year after the arrival of the inheritance from Urbino another notable batch of works passed into the Medici collection. As long ago as 1621 the death had occurred of Don Antonio de' Medici, Prince of Capistrano, the illegitimate son of Grand Duke Francesco I and Bianca Cappello. He had lived at the Casino di San Marco, built by Buontalenti, where he had gathered an important group of paintings that did not actually enter the gallery till 1632. It included above all two little panels by Fra Angelico; the three Mantegnas representing the *Circumcision, Ascension* and *Adoration of the Magi* (the latter then ascribed to Botticelli); Botticelli's small pictures of *Judith* and *the tent of Holofernes ;* Rosso's *Moses defending the Daughters of Jethro ;* Lavinia Fontana's *Noli me Tangere ;* and Titian's *Venus and Cupid* and *Portrait of Caterina Cornaro as St Catherine of Alexandria.*

An inventory of 1635 provides evidence that the Tribuna then contained Michelangelo's *Holy Family* tondo, Tintoretto's *Portrait of Jacopo Sansovino,* Lucas Cranach's *St George,* Dürer's *St Philip,* and

Amberger's *Portrait of Cornelius Gros*. They are all works that must have been added to the already enormous numbers in the Tribuna, if they did not replace ones that, as continued to happen in the following centuries, were transferred to the repository and then entered the other grand-ducal palaces and villas, according to the wishes of the sovereigns or their relatives.

Among the other rarities on display at that time was the rock-crystal casket, carved with the events of the Passion, that Valerio Belli had made for Pope Clement VII. Clement gave this casket to Francis I of France when Catherine de' Medici married the Duke of Orleans, who later became Henri II. It probably returned into Medici possession with the dowry of Christine of Lorraine on her marriage to Grand Duke Ferdinando II.

From the accounts of foreign travellers who had visited the gallery (John Evelyn's *Diary,* for example), which the Grand Dukes enjoyed showing off to royal guests and people interested in art, it appears that by the middle of the century marble statues on gilt or painted pedestals had been arranged in the south corridor; from there one entered the east corridor through a door flanked by two pillars adorned with trophies. These, which date back to the Flavian period, are now in the vestibule of the gallery. In the corridor there were statues and fifty busts from ancient times as well as some recent sculptures, including Michelangelo's *Bacchus* and Bernini's *Costanza Bonarelli ;* and in yet another was arranged the series of portraits copied from Paolo Giovio's collection. The room that had first been for the mathematical instruments now contained paintings, as did one of those following the Tribuna. There one saw the Titian *Venuses,* and the two small panels by Fra Angelico, along with the famous German Cabinet, made under the direction of Philip Hainhofer who took it to Innsbruck in 1628. It was given to the Grand Duke by Archduke Leopold of the Tyrol. Then came the three rooms of the armoury.

As early as about 1640 Ferdinando II was planning to decorate the five big rooms of the living quarters on the first floor of the Palazzo Pitti with frescoes. All but one of these rooms had been added in two phases to the original plan, on the initiative of Cosimo II and of Ferdinando himself, by the architects Giulio and Alfonso Parigi, who enhanced their splendour with an abundance of stucco and gilt decor-

THE ROOM OF JUPITER IN THE PALAZZO PITTI

ations. Each room was dedicated to a planet, indicating the five virtues needed by a ruler and possessed by Cosimo I. The first, of Venus, alluded to kindness, the second, of Apollo, to lofty splendour, the third, of Mars, to firmness in legislation, the fourth, of Jupiter, to regal majesty and the reward of merit, and the fifth, of Saturn, to prudence and the possession of deep knowledge. The devising of this glorification of Cosimo I, which was an idea of Francesco Rondinelli's, was supervised by Michelangelo Buonarroti the Younger and entrusted to Pietro da Cortona, who had painted frescoes for the Stove Room at the palace with the four ages of the world. In 1641 he painted the Venus Room, assisted on the stuccos of his own design by Cosimo Salvestrini, who directed their execution and organized the ornamenting with Medici busts. At the end of 1643 Pietro began another room, probably that of Jupiter, which was ready by the end of 1645. He started the Mars Room in 1646, and in 1647 that of Apollo, which he left unfinished. He did, however, prepare the cartoons in Rome, where he had returned, and the actual painting was done in 1659-60 by his pupil Ciro Ferri, who then decorated the Saturn Room with cartoons of his own during 1663-65. On this magnificent complex, in which the stuccos and cornices combine indissolubly with the frescoes, Pietro lavished all his powers of invention, achieving an effect of pomp vitality that must have had a considerable influence on contemporary artists, and not just those of Florence.

Grand Duke Ferdinando (and possibly his predecessor too) certainly intended to put the best paintings of the palace in these rooms, whether they were scattered in the apartments of the various princes or already arranged so as almost to form a gallery. This was not achieved, however, until the end of the century, by Ferdinando's successor. Even after this transfer, pictures continued as before to move between the Uffizi and the Palazzo Pitti.

THE ROOM OF MARS IN THE PALAZZO PITTI

Just as much interest in art was taken by other contemporary members of the Medici family, including Ferdinando's uncle, Cardinal Carlo, and the Grand Duke's brothers, Cardinal Giovancarlo and Prince Mattia, whose personal collections all passed at their death into the gallery.

Raised to the purple by Paul I in 1615, Protector of Spain in 1635, and Dean of the Sacred College in 1652, Cardinal Carlo played an important role in Papal politics, especially during the conclaves. But he never gave up collecting paintings and sculptures at his home in the Casino di San Marco, and when he died in 1666, many of these entered the gallery. Among his favourites were the painters of the early Renaissance. Botticelli was represented by his *Portrait of a Man with a Medal* (Uffizi); Fra Bartolommeo by the paintings of the risen Christ with two Prophets, which Carlo had brought from the friars of the Annunziata; Piero di Cosimo by the three panels showing the story of Perseus and Andromeda; Franciabigio by the *Madonna del Pozzo,* and Andrea del Sarto by the *Annunciation* purchased from the abbey at San Godenzo.

The Cardinal had as much feeling for the art of his own century, in that he also obtained Bernardo Strozzi's *Christ and the Pharisees* (Uffizi); *Christ and the Pharisee* and *Christ disputing with the Elders* from the school of Caravaggio; and Guido Reni's painting of *Bradamante and Fiordispina at the Spring.* Then, of great importance was the entry into the gallery of Rogier van der Weyden's *Entombment,* which, as we have seen, was in the collection of Lorenzo the Magnificent.

When Prince Mattia died in 1668 the gallery acquired, besides various paintings, a collection of astronomical instruments and a very remarkable group of ivories that he had found in Germany and other parts to which his soldiering had taken him as the head of the Grand Duchy's armed forces. Unfortunately not a great many of these ivories are still preserved at the Palazzo Pitti. Amongst the paintings were the 'four big landscapes with battles', in which Borgognone represented four of the Prince's most heroic deeds in Germany and Tuscany. They adorned a room of his villa at Lappeggi. One of them shows the assault on the fortress of Radicofani and another perhaps the Battle of Mongiovino, which on 4 September 1643 brought to an end the struggle between Ferdinando II and the Barberini.

In 1670, two years after Prince Mattia, Ferdinando died, and the government passed into the hands of his son Cosimo III. He was married then to Louise d'Orléans, the sister of Mlle de Montpensier, and daughter of Gaston d'Orléans, brother of the King of France; but the marriage proved extremely unsuccessful, and after a few years he was obliged to let her return to France, where she remained. Cosimo was a pious and religious man, who proved himself the worthy successor of his ancestors where the gallery and his artistic heritage were concerned.

In the first year of his reign another notable masterpiece of painting joined the others : Leonardo's *Adoration of the Magi*. Left unfinished by the artist, and then not placed in the church for which it had been commissioned, this had ended up, after various adventures, in the possession of Don Antonio de' Medici. But instead of being included in his legacy, it had remained at the home of his son Giulio, who, when he died, left it to the gallery. During his youth Cosimo had been sent on a tour of Europe accompanied by Lorenzo Magalotti, a learned and well-read Florentine. These travels probably account for the fact that at this time many Flemish and Dutch paintings entered the gallery, including Lucas van Leyden's *Crowning with Thorns,* then attributed to Dürer; Jan van der Heyden's view of Amsterdam town hall, which Cosimo acquired in 1678; the paintings of an old man in love (1673) and the artist's family (1675) done for the Grand Duke by Frans van Mieris; and Adriaen van der Werff's *Judgment of Solomon,* ordered for Cosimo by the Elector Palatine. To these can be added many other works by contemporary artists from the Netherlands appearing for the first time in the inventories made during this period; Caspar Netsche's *Sacrifice to Love* and *Offering to Venus;* a landscape by Anthonio Waterloo and Cornelis van Poelenburgh's *Finding of Moses* (both the latter then given to Paul Brill); Godfried Schalcken's *Woman Sewing;* Gabriel Metsu's *Woman tuning a Lute;* Gerard Dou's *Pancake Seller;* Frans van Mieris' *Beer Drinkers;* Gerard ter Borch's *Woman Drinking;* and Cornelis Bega's *Man playing the Mandolin* and *Man playing the Lute.*

In 1675 the death occurred of Ferdinando II's brother Leopoldo, who first as a prince and then from 1667 as a cardinal, had renewed in the broadest sense the patronage by then traditional in the family. He did so partly through his love and protection of the sciences, which he himself studied. With his brother, he prompted the foundation of the Accademia del Cimento (1657), of which he was president for ten years. But he also did so through his administrative work, chiefly in the field of land reclamation. By always allotting a considerable part of his income to the purchase of works of art, above all paintings and sculpture, he succeeded in gathering together a great many notable pieces that bear witness to his zeal for collecting, his intelligent taste, and his generosity. Among the works then on display in the Uffizi and Pitti galleries, the fifteenth-century masterpieces from his collection include Botticelli's *Madonna of the Pomegranate* ; the tondo by Francesco Botticini, at that time attributed to Botticelli; Piero del Pollaiuolo's *St Jerome* ; Filippino Lippi's *Portrait of an Old Man,* once ascribed to Masaccio; Piero di Cosimo's *Immaculate Conception,* and Perugino's *Virgin and Child with Angels.* For the sixteenth century one can cite Raphael's *Portrait of Tommaso Inghirami* ; works by Florentine artists such as Lorenzo di Credi, Agnolo Bronzino, Franciabigio, Pontormo, and Cecchino Salviati; Ferrarese works by Garofalo, Lodivico Mazzolino, and Dosso Dossi; and works by Annibale Carracci of Bologna, Bartolommeo Schedoni and Parmigianino of Emilia, Giampietrino of Lombardy, and Baroccio of the Marches.

More than half the paintings in the galleries that come from his estate are by Veneto artists. For twenty years Leopoldo made use of a Florentine nobleman living at Venice, Paolo del Sera, who was himself a collector as well as a painter. Paolo bought him paintings and drawings with exceptionnally good judgement, as is attested by Ridolfi and by Boschini in *La carta del naveger pitoresco.* The Cardinal was thus able not only to secure Giorgones and Titians (the figure of a Knight of Malta then thought to be by Titian; the *Concert,* ascribed to him now; the *Portrait of the prelate Beccadelli,* and that of *Tommaso Mosti,* but to represent in his collection the whole of sixteenth-century Veneto painting, from Bonifacio Veronese to Lorenzo Lotto, from Boccaccino to Paolo Veronese and Paris Bordone, from Sebastiano del Piombo to Savoldo, Moroni, Tintoretto, Bassano and Schiavone. Of the painting of his own century, he owned the *Cupid*

Asleep, now at the Pitti, by Caravaggio; the *Good Fortune* by Bartolommeo Manfredi, but then ascribed to Valentin; the *Madonna of the
Swallow* and *St Peter* by Guercino; and his own portrait by Baciccio,
in which his distinctive face is rendered with the keen and vigorous
directness of observation typical of the artist. The Florentines were
represented by Cigoli's *St Francis in Adoration,* Cristofano Allori's
Judith and a *Madonna* by Giovanni di San Giovanni; the Venetians by
Feti and Lys; the Neapolitans by Salvator Rosa. As for foreign art,
Leopoldo's collection included, among other works, Albrecht Dürer's
portrait of his father, which went straight into the Tribuna; Rubens'
two portraits of the Dukes of Buckingham, and his *Three Graces ;*
many portraits by Sustermans, the Court Painter at Florence under
Ferdinando II; Claude Lorrain's *Landscape with Figures* and *Seaport,*
which are two of his best works, now in the Uffizi; and paintings by
Paul Brill, Willem van Aelst, Denys Calvaert, and Frans Pourbus the
Younger, all of them Flemish or Dutch artists who spent periods in
Italy at this time.

But Leopoldo's enthusiasm was not limited to paintings; he also
built up a large collection of original drawings by painters, sculptors
and architects from Italy and abroad, in which a good 470 artists were
represented. The collection was of such importance that it formed
the nucleus of the collection in the Gabinetto dei Disegni at the Uffizi.
It included some of the drawings that are mentioned in Vasari's
famous Book, many of which have, alas, been scattered among various
Italian and non-Italian collections. The Cardinal gathered together
several thousand items, whose ordering he entrusted to Filippo Baldinucci, the author of *Notizie dei professori del disegno.* On Leopoldo's
death this appointment was renewed by Cosimo III, and Baldinucci
carried out his task in a scientific manner, with the aim of distinguishing the different authors and schools chronologically. The
drawings were actually included in the gallery in 1700, and formed
one of the earliest public collections of this kind.

Leopoldo was also attracted to the study of coins and medals, of
which he likewise assembled a great number, and eventually had about
4,000, including 750 in gold. There were many extremely rare pieces,
and in some classes he more than doubled what the earlier Grand
Dukes had bought. Still more notable was the collection of antique

PORTRAIT OF GIORGIO VASARI

cameos and intaglios that he formed in under fifteen years; it at once became a source of information for scholars, such as Leonardo Agostini, who were concerned with the history of gem-engraving. Then, in the Cardinal's correspondence there are references to purchases of marbles, bronzes, ancient inscriptions, arms and also miniatures : a series of over five hundred small portraits was kept in a cabinet that still existed at the end of the eighteenth century.

But the most remarkable collection was the one of painters' self-portraits, which was to be the beginning of the famous array at the Uffizi. Cosimo III very soon put it on show in the gallery, and had a suitable room built for it off the west corridor. The comparatively few examples that, as we learn from Lomazzo, had been brought together by Grand Duke Ferdinando I were no doubt also assembled there. With this collection, as with that of the drawings, Leopoldo took special pains to make sure that what he had been offered was genuine, seeking the opinion of contemporary artists and even going so far as to send doubtful works away from Florence, to hear the views of whoever he thought was the best judge. These self-portraits were a particularly important contribution to the gallery, because from then on artists of every nation, whether asked or not, sent likenesses of themselves, in the belief that their presence in the gallery was something to be justly proud of. The gallery thus gained works by artists whom, for various reasons, it would not have been easy or even possible to represent. The marble statue by Giovanni Battista Foggini of the Cardinal seated with some papers in his hand was also placed in the room built on Cosimo's orders. At the back hung Pier Dandini's painting of Tuscany crowned with the virtues, which disappeared during the subsequent alterations to these rooms.

Cosimo gradually moved most of the Cardinal's collections from the Pitti, where he had lived, to the Uffizi, so that they should immediately become known to visitors. He also enriched and embellished the gallery in other ways. Early in his reign he had various statues — among them a Hellenistic reclining *Apollo* and a *Mars* — brought from the Palazzo Pitti and the Boboli Gardens to improve the look of the west corridor, which, as the last to be adapted, was still sparsely adorned. He also saw to it that the series of famous men begun by Cosimo I was continued; and he had a room prepared for the collection of medals, which grew enormously in number during his reign. At his request Giandomenico Ferretti painted on the ceiling the story of Prometheus, with Anna Maria Lodovica of Tuscany as Minerva; but these decorations also disappeared when the rooms were being altered. In 1679 Cosimo acquired a collection of over thirteen thousand medals, and two years later he obtained another group, from Cardinal Massimo. To rearrange the medal room he called in Father Enrico Noris, whom he had made a professor at Pisa University. Noris took a long time over this, and more than once had occasion to write about exceptionally rare specimens, just as Francesco

APOLLO

Mezzabara Birago, Giovanni Foy Vaillant, and Anselmo Bandurio
did later. It was also under Cosimo III that the opening volume
was published of Thomas Dempster's *De Etruria Regali,* which is the
first manifestation of a new branch of study : Etruscology.

The entrance to the gallery at that time lay through the so-called
Door of Petitions, where the Via Lambertesca leads into the Piazzale
of the Uffizi, and at the end of the stairway Cosimo built a vestibule,

which was subsequently adorned with inscriptions, statues and marble bas-reliefs. It was during this period too, that the transfer began of the antiquities still at the Villa Medici in Rome. Some of the most famous marbles, such as the Medici *Venus*, the so-called *Knife-grinder*, and the *Wrestlers*, arrived in 1677; and as the sculptor Ercole Ferrata was in Florence then, he was appointed to carry out the few restorations that the marbles needed. This led to a similar commission for work on all the statues in the gallery, and after Ferrata had spent some time on the job he was succeeded by Giuseppe Piamontini, a pupil of his, and by Francesco Franchi. During these years Cardinal Leopoldo also acquired the huge bust of Antinous, discovered in 1671 and restored by Paolo Naldini and Ciro Ferri, while Canon Apollonio Bassetti's legacy brought the ivory diptych of the Consul Basil, the Faun mask, then thought to be Michelangelo's earliest work (it disappeared during the war), and a wax model ascribed to Michelangelo, along with marbles, drawings, medals and coins.

The heir to Cosimo's throne was his son Ferdinando, who had the title of Grand Prince of Tuscany, and was an ardent collector of paintings. But he died before his father, in 1713, and so his collection, which also contained drawings, prints, bronzes, arms, gems and medals, passed into the gallery. The most notable part of it was undoubtedly the paintings. These included Andrea del Sarto's *Madonna of the Harpies*, which Ferdinando obtained from the nuns of San Francesco at Florence; Fra Bartolommeo's *St Mark* and his painting of the *Virgin with St George and other Saints*, which had both been in the church of San Marco, as well as the other painting of the *Madonna with Florentine Saints*, which he prepared for the council chamber in the Palazzo della Signoria but left unfinished; and Carletto Caliari's *Miracle of St Fridigian*, in which the saint is shown checking the river Serchio near Castelfranco di Sotto. Venetian painting was represented by the *Three Ages of Man*, which is Giorgionesque if not actually by Giorgione himself; two Titian portraits (the anatomist Andreas Vesalius and, probably, Federigo Gonzaga); Tintoretto's portrait of Luigi Cornaro and a *Deposition* from his school; and Francesco Bassano's *St Catherine*. Parmigianino's so-called *Madonna with the long Neck*, which had been bought from the Servite fathers of Parma, represented Emilian painting. The seventeenth-century works collected by the

THE KNIFE-GRINDER

Grand Prince are also proof of his sound judgement, from Annibale
Carracci's *Christ in Glory* to Guido Reni's *Bacchus;* from Cagnacci's
Assumption of St Mary Magdalen to Orazio Riminaldi's *Cupid the Artist,*
Simone's *St Andrew,* and Alessandro Tarini's *Adam and Eve ;* from
Guercino's *St Sebastian* to Carlo Maratta's *Virgin appearing to St Filippo
Neri,* Cigoli's *Supper at Emmaus,* Carlo Dolci's *Diogenes,* and Volterrano's *Venal Love* and *Cupid Asleep.* As for foreign paintings, there
was the one by Rubens showing *Nymphs surprised by Satyrs,* the *Portrait of Cosimo III as a child* by Sustermans, and two still-lifes by Willem van Aelst. When making purchases Ferdinando took the advice
of painters like the Genoese Niccolò Cassana, with whom he was
repeatedly in touch over gathering small pictures of every school to
adorn a small private room then under preparation in the villa of
Poggio a Caiano; or like the Bolognese Giuseppe Maria Crespi, with

whom he regularly had informal discussions on many topics relating to art. One should also mention that it was Ferdinando who set about having the pictures owned by his family drawn and etched, a project that was only partly realized.

GIANGASTONE AND THE END OF THE LINE OF MEDICI

The reign of Giangastone, the second son of Cosimo III, who succeeded his father in 1723, was not so favourable to the gallery. We know that in 1731 he acquired over three hundred engraved gems from the collection of Abbot Piero Andreo Andreini, and that in making this purchase he took advice from Sebastiano Bianchi, whom his father had already put in charge of the gem and medal room. Meanwhile, partly through the generosity with which the Grand Dukes let

THE WRESTLERS

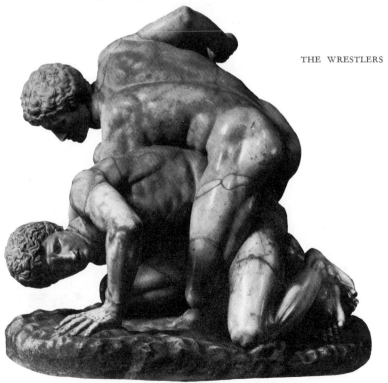

people visit their collections, the interest taken by scholars in the antiquities at the gallery was constantly growing. It led to the issue of works in which many of these ancient things were published and thus made generally familiar. At that time the men chiefly responsible for this were Anton Francesco Gori, who in his books about the ancient inscriptions in Tuscany first published those preserved at the gallery, and Marquis Scipione Maffei, who singled out the pieces, among those made known by Gori, about whose authenticity he had doubts, exercizing a severe critical judgement of great value to philology. In other writings he commented on many items from the medal room and gem collection, referring particularly to the modern cameos. It was a society of Florentine nobles that undertook the publication of a ten-volume work dealing with all the most valuable antiquities at the gallery and the other museums in Florence, except for inscriptions and bas-reliefs. The leader of the enterprise was Senator Filippo Buonarroti, who made use of Sebastiano Bianchi and Gori. This work began to come out in 1731, with the volumes on the gems, which were followed years later by those on the medallions, and finally by those on the portraits of the painters. Gori supplied the explanatory texts for the individual plates, and with the appearance in 1737 of the volumes about the Etruscan Museum he may be said worthily to have carried out his task of being the first commentator on the gallery's ancient things, apart from the paintings.

Giangastone, the last male representative of the Medici family, died in 1737.

ANNA MARIA LODOVICA AND THE FAMILY PACT

Giangastone's sister, Anna Maria Lodovica, had married the Elector Palatine, Johann Wilhelm. When she was widowed as early as 1716 she returned to Florence, bringing with her a large number of good Flemish paintings, especially ones by Adriaen van der Werff, which were added to others she had sent her father as a gift the previous year. She also brought many engraved gems, coins, and medals in gold and silver of the German princes, which were also admitted into the gallery. When her brother died, Anna Maria Lodovica was left as the sole surviving member of the Medici family, and in a manner worthy of her best forefathers she brought to a conclusion the work they had begun a few centuries earlier.

It was necessary to call upon Duke Francis of Lorraine to succeed the Medici. In fact Giangastone's successor had already been named during his lifetime in the person of the Infante Don Carlos, second son of the King of Spain who, according to the agreement between Charles V and Clement VII, reserved the right to direct the succession. Soon afterwards, however, Don Carlos renounced Tuscany, upon the conquest of the kingdom of the Two Sicilies. Without consulting Giangastone, who was whiling away what remained of his life in debauchery, Francis of Lorraine was named in his place, in compensation for his own estates now reunited with France. Anna Maria Lodovica concluded the so-called Family Pact with him, which ensured the future of the Medici collections. Article Three reads : ' Her Serene Highness the Electoress now cedes, gives, and transfers to H.R.H., for him and for his successors as Grand Duke, all the furniture, effects, and rarities of the estate of her brother His Serene Highness the Grand Duke, such as galleries, paintings and statues, libraries, jewels, and other valuable things like the holy relics and reliquaries and their ornaments in the chapel of the Royal Palace, which H.R.H. pledges himself to preserve on the express condition that none of what is for the adornment of the state and the benefit of the public, and to attract the interest of foreigners, shall be transported or taken away from the capital and the state of the Grand Duchy '.

Through this agreement Anna Maria Lodovica showed that she had much more than ' some gleam of Medici greatness ', which is what certain contemporaries grudgingly accorded her; and in the negotiations leading up to it she also showed considerable energy and skill, which helped to make the minor conditions as unburdensome as possible. Drawn up on 15 July 1737, the pact was signed in Vienna on 27 November of the same year, and thus assured Florence the enjoyment for ever of the collections gathered in three centuries by the Medici family. With this agreement the Uffizi gallery, which, through the generosity of the rulers, had been visited by Italians and foreigners almost from its foundation, became a truly public gallery and the property of the Tuscan state.

ANDREA DEL CASTAGNO. FARINATA DEGLI UBERTI

The House of Lorraine

FRANCIS OF LORRAINE, GRAND DUKE OF TUSCANY AND A CONNOISSEUR
OF ANTIQUITIES

Francis of Lorraine did not stay in Tuscany for long; he spent most
of the time in Vienna, even before he was made Emperor in 1745.
But he did not omit to send the gallery pictures, bronzes and medallions. On the death of Sebastiano Bianchi in 1738, Antonio Cocchi
was appointed official antiquary and keeper of the gem and medal
room. When he died in 1758, his son Raimondo succeeded him.
During these years the first guide to the gallery was published,
written by Giuseppe Bianchi, its first curator. Under Grand Duke Francis the laws were brought back into force that related to the export
of art objects and to any finds made in the course of excavations. First
formulated by Cosimo I, these laws had been reconfirmed in 1602
by Ferdinando I. The Tuscan government was led to take further steps
by the frequent discoveries of ancient things during excavations at
many sites in the region, such as the one at Volterra, which had attracted the sovereign's attention, as well as those elsewhere that had already
produced large quantities of Roman coins, bronze cult figures, and
fragments of pottery. On the other hand, Francis did not fail to buy
coins and bronzes when he had the chance. He also wanted to have
pen drawings made of the whole gallery in its present state, under the

57

direction of Father De Greys. At the same time Ignazio Orsini had the ceiling of the west corridor drawn and engraved on copper. Unfortunately a fire in 1762 did serious damage to the end of the west corridor, destroying twelve sections of the painted ceiling, nine portraits, six statues, and a few busts, as well as injuring others.

PIETRO LEOPOLDO

It was Francis' successor Pietro Leopoldo, who, having mounted the throne in 1765, saw to the repairs and commissioned Giuseppe del Moro, Giuliano Traballesi, Giuseppe Terreni and Agostino Fortini to decorate the reconstructed ceiling. In the Medici tradition, he added a small collection of self-portraits which the engraver Abbot Antonio Pazzi assembled and published in two volumes.

In 1769 the post of director of the gallery was created, and it was filled by Canon Giuseppe Querci, who, according to the sovereign's wishes, tried to improve the arrangement of the material. Pietro Leopoldo wanted the finest and most rare things in the grand-ducal palaces and villas to enter the gallery, and he ordered the removal to Florence of the figures representing the story of Niobe, the Hellenistic copy of Doidalsas's *Aphrodite,* the young *Apollo* of the Tribuna, and Giambologna's *Mercury,* which were then still at the Villa Medici in Rome. He also had the most notable paintings transferred from some offices of the civic authorities, paintings that included Fra Angelico's tabernacle of the Arte dei Linaiuoli and Empoli's painting of *St Ivo,* the protector of orphans. Then he bought or received as gifts such valuable works as the portrait of Michelangelo, Guercino's *Samian Sibyl,* and Giovanni Martinelli's *Belshazzar's Feast.* From the Galluzzi family of Volterra he purchased their entire collection of Etruscan objects found in that district. Shortly afterwards he obtained the fifth-century votive shield of the Ardaburi, discovered at Cosa, followed by Ignazio Orsini's collection of mediaeval and modern coins and medals. At this time many works entered the gallery that had been in the Gaddi gallery, above all drawings, prints, and a few excellent antique sculptures, among which the Hellenistic *Torso of a Faun* is especially valuable, as are some busts that may represent Imperial personages, and Donatello's puzzling *Cupid* (or Attis).

GIOVANNI DA BOLOGNA. MERCURY

It was in Pietro Leopoldo's day that the gallery parted company for good with the collections of scientific specimens and instruments. Of the greatest interest, these had been added to by the various Grand Dukes, but their proper place was no longer beside the art treasures. So a natural science room was established, where all this valuable material could be concentrated. Unfortunately, still with the aim of procuring more space for the works of art, some porcelain and arms were thrown out, and this began the almost complete dispersal of the Medici armoury, which would have been exceptionally interesting

A DAUGHTER OF NIOBE

today. Pietro Leopoldo is also to be credited with the building of the room for gems and the Niobe Room, which was designed by Gaspare Paoletti and adorned with stuccos by Grato Albertolli, from the Lugano region.

The succeeding directors at that period — first Raimondo Cocchi, who took Querci's place in 1773, and then Giuseppe Pelli in 1775 — had the sovereign's full support over a plan to achieve a logical and final rearrangement of the gallery. Thought out by the antiquary Luigi Lanzi, this was relized during 1780-82.

It was then that the old entrance from the Via Lambertesca was replaced by the present one from the east portico of the Uffizi, up Vasari's staircase to the first floor and then up two newly constructed flights leading to a rectangular space followed by the present vestibule, which was decorated with antique sculptures. Along the walls of the corridors, now fully adorned with statues and busts, were disposed paintings of all the Italian and foreign schools, in chronological order, while the sculptures and paintings occupied, besides the Tribuna, all the neighbouring rooms, which also included the one for antique vessels and the one for prints and drawings. The gems were arranged in the room specially built for them (now reserved for the miniatures instead), and the Niobe group was set up in the magnificent room already mentioned. Finally, at the end of the west corridor, two small rooms housed the ancient and modern bronzes, while the Etruscan Museum was sited with a view over the terrace above the Loggia della Signoria.

FERDINANDO III AND THE NAPOLEONIC CONSFISCATIONS

When Pietro Leopoldo mounted the Imperial throne in 1790, he was succeeded in Tuscany by his second son, Ferdinando III. Meanwhile the collections of the gallery were continuing to grow. In 1792 a purchase was made in Paris of works by seventeenth-century French painters, including Laurent de La Hire, Charles Lebrun, Pierre Mignard, and Alexis Grimou. The following year an exchange of pictures with the Vienna gallery was agreed upon in a way that may now be considered highly advantageous to Florence. The Uffizi made over an *Isaiah* by Fra Bartolommeo, a *Virgin and Child with the Infant St John* by Andrea del Sarto, a *Holy Family with St Elizabeth and the Infant St John* by Bronzino, the *Portrait of a Religious* by Baroccio, a *St Luke* by Volterrano, and a *Virgin and Child* by Carlo Dolci. In return it received twenty-three works including Giovanni Bellini's

Sacred Allegory, Titian's *Virgin and Child with the Infant St John and St Anthony Abbot* and his *Flora,* a Palma Vecchio *Virgin and Child,* Veronese's *Esther and Ahasuerus,* and Dürer's *Adoration of the Magi.*

French rule very soon led to distressing impairments of the gallery. It was in vain that the director Tommaso Puccini took the Medici *Venus* to Palermo, along with the cameos and other precious objects : the First Consul obtained it from King Ferdinand IV of the Two Sicilies and had it brought to Paris, where sixty-three paintings and twenty-seven tables inlaid with Florentine mosaic from the Palazzo Pitti had already been sent. This was a very grave decimation of the gallery's contents, since it included five Rubens, four Titians, and seven Raphaels, and the others carried off were also carefully chosen from among the best. The second pillage in 1810 only concerned the paintings that had been gathered together at the Academy of Fine Arts from the suppressed religious houses and did not yet form part of the gallery. They comprised Fra Angelico's *Coronation of the Virgin,* a Botticelli *Madonna,* Raffaellino del Garbo's *Coronation of the Virgin,* Andrea del Castagno's *St John the Baptist with two Monks,* a *Nativity* by Fra Filippo Lippi, a *Virgin and Child with Saints* by Cosimo Ros-selli, a *Visitation* by Domenico Ghirlandaio, a *Virgin and Child with Saints* by Lorenzo di Credi, and a *Presentation in the Temple* by Gentile da Fabriano. To these were added a fourteenth-century sculpture and various paintings taken from Pisa. In 1815 some of the works that had been removed came back to Florence, including the Medici *Venus,* which was restored to its place in the Tribuna, where Canova's *Venus Italica* had been substituted for it. But seven paintings and nine tables from the gallery at the Palazzo Pitti did not return, nor did any of the pictures taken away in 1810. It is painful to read in the report of the recovery commission, which included Senator Giovanni degli Alessandri, Puccini's successor as director, that these had been left at the insistence of the French government, but also that, as they were second-rate works and extremely heavy, being on panel, it had been considered inadvisable to meet the cost of packing and transport.

In 1798 the gallery at the Palazzo Pitti had also been given a perma-nent arrangement. Since the time when Cosimo III had disposed it in the rooms frescoed for his predecessor, it had extended to other rooms on the first floor, partly in connection with the subsequent enlargements of the palace itself. It had come to include, that is to say, the Stove Rooms, which Pietro da Cortona had painted with the four ages of the world before he did the others, the one known as the Gallery, decorated by Bernardino Poccetti, and those of the Volterano Suite — so-called because of his fresco in the Allegories Room — as well as a few other intermediate ones. At the start of the nineteenth century another, directly following those with frescoes by Pietro da Cortona, was prepared, and it took the name of the Iliad Room owing to the frescoes of episodes from the Trojan epic that Sabatelli painted there in 1819. Also, the remaining rooms behind those with windows in the façade had their ceilings decorated. The Fine Arts Room was adorned by Domenico Podestà, the Hercules Room by Pietro Benvenuti, the Aurora Room by Gaspare Martellini, the Berenice Room by Giuseppe Bezzuoli with Titus abandoning Berenice, the Psyche Room by Giuseppe Collignon, the Ark Room and the Music Room by Luigi Ademollo, the latter with frescoes referring to the liberation of Vienna, the Prometheus Room by Giuseppe Collignon, the Justice Room by Antonio Fedi with Justice between Mercury and Peace, the Flora Room and the Putti Room by Antonio Marini, the Ulysses Room by Gaspare Martinelli with a fresco alluding to Ferdinando III's return, and the Education of Jupiter Room by Luigi Catani. Many of the Flemish pictures brought by the Electoress Palatine had remained in the gallery, and Francesco II had added others. Grand Duke Ferdinando III put Raphael's famous *Madonna of the Grand Duke* there, and in 1818 he also acquired a selection of paintings from the Gerini gallery, including a Rembrandt *Self-Portrait,* Van Dyck's *Rest on the Flight,* two Salvator Rosas, and Guercino's *St Sebastian.* Later on Leopoldo III obtained the portraits of Agnolo and Maddalena Doni by Raphael. The gallery, to which Raphael's *Portrait of Leo X* and *Madonna of the Chair* had come from the Uffizi, thus became increasingly important, bringing together, among other works, no less then eleven Raphaels, thirteen Titians, and nine Rubens.

LEOPOLDO II

Ferdinando III was succeeded by Leopoldo II, but the new sovereign took just as much interest in the gallery, whose successive directors

DESIDERIO DA SETTIGNANO. BUST OF A CHILD

constantly improved its arrangements and worked on a new inventory, which was completed in 1825. In accordance with the awakening of interest in Egyptology that followed Napoleon's expedition, the Nizzoli collection was purchased in 1824, and the material gathered by the Rosellini expedition, sent out by the Florentine government, joined it after 1828. As a result it was decided, in view of the already excessive crowding of the art treasures at the gallery, to create an Egyptian museum elsewhere. Its home was the former church of Santa Caterina and then the convent of the Foligno nuns in the Via Faenza. Eventually the paintings by contemporary artists were hung in the Palazzo della Crocetta, and thus the slow dispersal leading, after several decades, to the gallery's present aspect was continued.

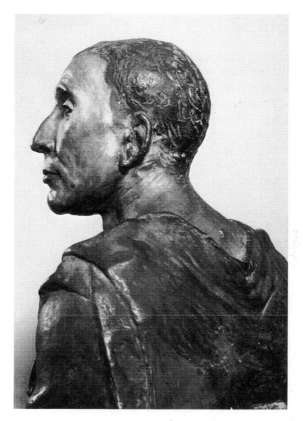

DONATELLO. NICCOLÒ DA UZZANO

THE KINGDOM OF ITALY AND THE HOUSE OF SAVOY

The dispersal took place above all after the fall of the Lorraine dynasty, between 1860 and 1870, with the founding of the Museo Nazionale in the Palazzo del Podestà or Bargello, which gradually received all the post-antique sculptures that had been in the gallery, as well as all the minor art objects, and with the removal of the Etruscan Museum to the place where the Egyptian Museum had previously been. Then came the creation of a museum in the Palazzo della Crocetta, where all the archaeological material, including the Egyptian and Etruscan, was concentrated, with the sole exception of the classical sculptures that remained in the Uffizi.

At the same time the gallery continued to be enriched with notable works. From the church of Ognissanti came the Giovanni da Milano polyptych and from Santa Lucia de' Magnoli the painting by Domenico Veneziano; to the gem collection was added the collection bequeathed by Guglielmo Currie, which comprised about five hundred cameos and intaglios; from a church in the Val d'Elsa arrived the big Lorenzo Monaco polyptych with the *Adoration of the Magi*. It was then that the distinctive corridor built by Vasari to link the Uffizi with the Pitti was opened to the public. In it was displayed part of the drawing collection, which during those very years received about thirteen thousand pieces from Emilio Santarelli.

The suppression of the religious orders that had already occurred under Pietro Leopoldo and Napoleon had resulted in the founding of a gallery at the Academy of Fine Arts, which was given charge of the works taken from the monasteries and convents. In 1866 a further suppression not only enriched this gallery but also led to the creation of a museum in the friary of San Marco, which preserved other works of art besides the Fra Angelico frescoes. Not many of the paintings from the suppressed houses entered the Uffizi, but among those that did were Lorenzo Monaco's triptych and Leonardo's *Annunciation* from the Florentine monastery of Monteoliveto, Cosimo Rosselli's *Virgin and Child* and Bacchiacca's *Crucifixion* from the monastery of Santa Maria Maddalena de' Pazzi, and Sogliani's *Trinity* from Sant' Iacopo Soprana. Afterwards, in the course of several reorderings that the gallery owed partly to its enlargement through the construction of new rooms on the site of the old Medici theatre, many paintings were, at various times, moved from the Accademia to the Uffizi. The result was a more complete panorama of Italian painting, and one that in particular remedied the obvious shortage of thirteenth and fourteenth-century works, which had only occasionally found a place in the original Medici collections, and for which there had been no special demand in the centuries that followed. But a great many masterpieces from the fifteenth century and after — naturally with religious subjects — were also introduced, and they show in full the development of, above all, Florentine and Tuscan painting.

At the beginning of the twentieth century a very important addition to the gallery came through the purchase of the art collection at

CORRIDOR IN THE UFFIZI

the hospital of Santa Maria Nuova. It included the famous Hugo van
der Goes triptych that Tommaso Portinari sent for the church of the
hospital founded by his ancestor.

At the end of the nineteenth century the gallery's arrangement
followed, if incompletely, the principle of display by single schools,
except, of course, for the self-portraits. It was this principle that
governed the various changes in position made by Enrico Ridolfi
and Corrado Ricci in order to improve the layout. But the achieve-
ment of an order combining a strictly scientific presentation with
regard for the gallery's distinctive original settings was the work of
Giovanni Poggi, who spent almost forty years as director of the gallery
and then as superintendent. He removed the paintings from the corridors, replacing them by the many tapestries woven in Florence and

ROOM IN THE UFFIZI

abroad. Not the least glory of the grand-ducal artistic heritage, these were alternated with the antique sculptures, which also acquired a room at the beginning of the east corridor, and in this way the corridors of the sixteenth-century fabric were given a particularly impressive appearance. Poggi also organized the chronological arrangement of the paintings by single schools, transferring from the Accademia all those that could help to make it as complete as possible. After the Second World War a large hall built out of the upper part of a room belonging to the Record Office below was added to the gallery, and a purely chronological arrangement replaced the one by schools.

The Pitti gallery, on the other hand, did not undergo any important changes, even in its layout, after the fall of the Lorraine dynasty. After the last war, too, it was reopened without radical alterations, the idea being to let it retain its special character as a court gallery.

Thus, the two galleries form a remarkable whole, and they even complement one another. The Uffizi has a collection of masterpieces that offers an almost complete view of Italian painting, together with a series of first-rate non-Italian works. The Pitti is also full of masterpieces, but its contents are limited, with very few exceptions, to sixteenth-and seventeenth-century paintings; it gives an idea of the taste that prevailed in the centuries of its formation, and it is almost the last surviving example of a sovereign's gallery.

ROOM IN THE UFFIZI

Other Florentine Museums

It has already been emphasized, and the reader may see for himself from this brief introduction, that the Medici and their successors of the House of Lorraine did not only collect paintings. They systematically assembled every form of art : sculpture, faïence, vases, *pietra dura,* arms and armour, rare materials. A certain proportion was left in the Uffizi and Pitti, in order to preserve the original character of the galleries, but other museums had to be created in order to house the majority of these objects.

Only a few of the ancient marble sculptures, for instance, have been left in the Uffizi. Most of them, with almost all the Egyptian and Etruscan objects, the Greek and Roman bronzes, the vase and coin collections, the ancient cameos and intaglios, were sent in 1880 to the Palazzo Crocetta, where they formed the Museo Archeologico.

The mediaeval and modern collections belonging to the Uffizi went, from 1865 on, to create the Museo Nazionale in the old Palazzo del Podestà, or Bargello, which was restored at that time. First to go were the old arms, all that remained of the rich Medici armoury whose sad fate has been mentioned. They were followed by the works in ivory and amber, and then by the very important collection of Urbino faïence

MICHELANGELO. THE PALESTRINA PIETÀ

(most of which was given to the Medici by the Dukes of Urbino, or was part of the Della Rovere legacy). The new museum also received a large number of post-mediaeval bronzes and, about ten years later, all the post-mediaeval sculpture, consisting of a notable group of masterpieces by Donatello, Della Robbia, Desiderio da Settignano, Matteo Civitali, Michelangelo, and many others. The Medici medal collection and the collection of Florentine coins from the Mint also went to the Bargello.

The Accademia gallery, which has already been mentioned, is famous above all today for the works by Michelangelo exhibited

MICHELANGELO.   DAVID

there. In 1873 his *David* was taken from the Piazza della Signoria and sent to the gallery, where the architect Emilio de Fabris built the existing apsed hall for it in 1882. This made it possible to unite in the same surroundings other works by Michelangelo, such as the *St Matthew,* the four unfinished *Prisoners* for the tomb of Julius II, which, presented by Michelangelo's nephew Leonardo Buonarroti to Cosimo I, had been used as atlantes in Buontalenti's grotto in the Boboli gardens, where they were replaced in 1908 by casts; and then, after the last war, the Palestrina *Pietà,* acquired from the Barberini family.

The Michelangelos were joined in 1911 by the original plaster model for Giambologna's *Rape of the Sabine Women,* which is under the Loggia della Signoria in the piazza of the same name, and by one for his *Virtue overpowering Vice,* now at the Bargello.

The Accademia dates back to the sixteenth century. It was Cosimo I who, as early as 1562-63, at the suggestion of Montorsoli, Vasari and others, laid the foundations for an Academy of Fine Arts, which was destined to replace the Company of St Luke (Patron Saint of Painters and Drawers). Cosimo ordered that all works done in honour of St

Luke and the Holy Trinity, or in memory of past great masters, should remain the property of the Accademia, which also had a right to the sample works shown by teachers aspiring to become academicians. The Accademia's role was consequently at first purely instructive, and its collection was intended to serve as a model for students and future artists. The collection grew steadily, acquiring some mediocre works, but also more valuable ones, such as the 'clay model with an armature' by Michelangelo, which Bartolommeo Ammannati, who had received it as a present from Cosimo I, gave to the Accademia in 1583. By the nineteenth century the origin of the model has been forgotten, but then its importance was recognized again, and it went back on show in the gallery, where it can still be seen today. Unfortunately, however, many of these works were soon dispersed—sold, given away, or destroyed, either because the Accademia could no longer keep them on its own premises, or in order to raise funds.

For a while the Accademia sheltered a collection of portraits of great artists of the past (including *Beato Fra Angelico* by Carlo Dolci), and a collection of portraits of the gallery's directors, begun by Fran-

MICHELANGELO.   PRISONER

cesco Maria Ricasoli in 1596, but both collections were subsequently moved to the Uffizi. When Grand Duke Pietro Leopoldo I reformed the Accademia in 1784 and gave it its final seat in the former hospital of San Matteo on the Piazza di San Marco, the gallery consisted of many paintings, cartoons, drawings, and a few other art objects, which were joined in 1786 by another series of works which helped to complete the various schools already represented. The same year, Pietro Leopoldo's suppression of some confraternities and religious institutions, caused paintings of the early Florentine and Tuscan schools to pour into the gallery. Eventually, however, they were mostly transferred to the Uffizi and replaced by works of later periods.

When the French government completely abolished the religious orders in 1810, a further batch of religious paintings was entrusted to the Accademia, which overflowed into the ex-friary of San Marco.

The gallery thus came to own a wonderful collection of Tuscan works, set out chronologically from the twelfth century to 1841. It consisted of 260 paintings and 24 cartoons arranged in what had been the women's ward of the former hospital of San Matteo, and in three other rooms, one large and two small; then, from 1855, also in adjacent rooms of the suppressed nunnery of San Niccolò. Besides this gallery, the Accademia had the so-called Prize-winners' Gallery, which received the paintings, *bozzetti,* and drawings of the winners of the triennial competitions announced by the Accademia itself, and the yearly test pieces of scholarship-holders, studying outside Florence. From 1866 it also boasted a gallery of modern pictures made up of works acquired by the last Grand Duke, chosen at the annual shows of the Society for promoting the Fine Arts, or executed for contests.

During the last decade of the nineteenth century, the gallery had been given the name of Ancient and Modern Gallery, which it kept till 1918, when, in the general rearrangement of Florence's art heritage, it was radically transformed and was once more called the Accademia. Many of the old pictures were moved to the Uffizi, as essential to the latter's reorganization, and others were sent to the Accademia in exchange. These preserved its character as a collection of Tuscan work up to the sixteenth century.

At the same time the nineteenth-century paintings went to form a Gallery of Modern Art, which was housed rather unsatisfactorily on the second floor of the Palazzo Pitti. To this nucleus of paintings was added, by virtue of an agreement with the corporation of Florence, a collection of works that formerly belonged to the municipality, and also those left by Diego Martelli, a shrewd collector with good taste, attached to the Macchiaioli movement (a group of Tuscan painters at the end of the nineteenth century who renewed painting techniques, and employed a system of chromatic brushstrokes). The gallery thus contains a cross-section of the Classicists, the Romantics, and the new academicians of the Tuscan School; a wide representation of the Macchiaioli, which has been considerably extended by Leone Ambron's generous gift; a good basic collection of works by late nineteenth and early twentieth-century Tuscan artists; those works awarded the national Fiorino prize, and further legacies, such as the Ghiglia bequest of works mainly by Cristiano Banti, as well as of gifts like those from the Cenacolo dei XII Apostoli, a group of Florentine artists and writers.

The Fra Angelico Museum at the ex-friary of San Marco came into being more recently than the Accademia gallery. This friary had been united with the Academy of Fine Arts since the beginning of the nineteenth century, and in 1810 a store was made there for the works of art from the suppressed religious houses. After the next suppression, of 1866, it was decided to make it a museum and, suitably restored, it was opened to the public in 1869. The conventual building, raised by Michelozzo for Cosimo de' Medici between 1437 and the start of the next decade, is adorned with frescoes by Fra Angelico and his followers in the first cloister, the chapter room, the first-floor corridor, and every cell. Today it contains, in the hospice, all the works by Fra Angelico that used to be in the Florentine galleries, apart from the two remaining at the Uffizi (the *Coronation of the Virgin* and *Madonna of Pontassieve*). Also assembled in the museum are works by Fra Bartolommeo della Porta, who was likewise a friar at San Marco, and others. In the refectory is Domenico Ghirlandaio's *Last Supper*. This arrangement dates from the years just after the First World War, and it was somewhat improved in 1955 on the occasion of the five-hundredth anniversary of Fra Angelico's death. Michelozzo's library was returned to all its original splendour, some of the paintings were restored, the Della Robbia tabernacle was put

FRA ANGELICO. THE ADORATION OF THE MAGI

back in the wash room where it had been, and other rooms, too, regained their former simplicity, through the removal of works that had since accumulated in them. One can now see a fifteenth-century conventual building that is almost intact, in which the works of art created for it find again the atmosphere that inspired their authors.

The same principle also inspired at this period the founding of an Andrea del Castagno Museum in a refectory of the ex-monastery of Sant' Apollonia, where the artist had painted his finest group of frescoes. With these were hung other detached frescoes of his, from Florentine religious buildings, as well as those once in the Villa Carducci, then Pandolfini, at Legnaia, in the immediate neighbourhood of the city. The refectory was the only room of the monastery that had not undergone military occupation, and its restoration was consequently made easier. The frescoes above the *Last Supper (Resurrection, Crucifixion, Entombment)*, which were formerly very hard to decipher owing to their state of preservation, were detached and are now recognized as being among Andrea's greatest works and among the noblest creations of fifteenth-century Florence. They are accompanied by a *Pietà* from another room of the same monastery, but unfortunately it is damaged. The *Famous Men and Women* frescoes from the Villa Carducci were detached halfway through the nineteenth century. Acquired in 1852, they went in 1853 to the Museo Nazionale, then being created at the Bargello, and from there they were eventually moved to the refectory at Sant' Apollonia.

The restorations that are now being carried out by the Università degli Studi in the other rooms of the ex-monastery, will restore to the city one of the most notable conventual buildings of the period.

It is a characteristic of all the Florentine museums and galleries that they are contained in historic buildings. This is obvious in the case of the two principal galleries, which originated in the buildings they still occupy through the wishes of the rulers who brought them into being. The Uffizi was chosen by Francesco de' Medici for this purpose because of its proximity to the Palazzo della Signoria, and because of the opportunity provided by the top-floor corridors for setting out works of art. The Palazzo Pitti is the natural home of the gallery bearing the same name, in that it used to be the private gallery of the ruling family.

So it is with the Fra Angelico Museum, established in the ex-friary of San Marco where the artist worked, and with the Accademia gallery, which has remained next to the institution from which it issued. In the case of the Museo Nazionale, however, the selection of the Palazzo del Podestà goes back, as we have seen, to the nineteenth century, while for the museum of the old Florentine house created in the recently acquired Palazzo Davanzati, the choice is very suitable. It is natural that these buildings, which form such an essential and integral part of the panorama of Florentine culture, should be used, and it would be a shame to remove the collections which have been housed there during centuries.

It must be admitted, though, that the use of such buildings for galleries and museums poses certain problems and precludes, at least in part, the application of the most modern principles of museology, as they affect lighting, preservation and arrangement, since the

77

rooms cannot, or cannot fully, be adapted without altering the basic architectural structure. However unpopular the idea is to lovers of Florence, one cannot exclude the possibility of constructing new buildings to house the collections; it is, in fact, bound to happen to a certain extent when the profusion of works of art overflows the existing museums and makes it essential to create subsidiary buildings. This is particulary to be desired in the case of the Gallery of Modern Art, where the age of the palace raises problems of space and lighting making it almost impossible to show contemporary works in an appropriate setting.

THE PLATES

CIMABUE *(Cenni di Pepo)* (Mentioned 1240–1302)   *Florentine School*
THE MADONNA AND CHILD WITH SAINTS
(below, four half-length figures of Prophets)   Panel
Inv. No. 8343   Height 385 cm. (151⁵/₈″)
                                                  Width 223 cm. (87³/₄″)

This painting originally stood on the high altar of the Vallumbrosan church
of Santa Trinità at Florence. If it is accepted that Niccolò Pisano began
building the church in 1268, as has been claimed by Paatz and others, then
it follows that the picture could have been executed between that date and
1272, when the artist was active at Rome. But not all critics are agreed
on placing the *Madonna and Child* before the Assisi frescoes, which
followed the stay at Rome; for some see them rather as a result of these
frescoes, owing to the difference in their constructional character. Today
the prevailing view puts the *Madonna and Child* after 1280, round about
1285, and makes it the harbinger of the Assisi frescoes, which date from
about 1288–90. The painting was removed from the altar in 1472, when
it was replaced by Alesso Baldovinetti's *Trinity,* commissioned two years
earlier by the Gianfigliazzi and now in the Galleria dell'Accademia at
Florence. Yet this did not diminish its renoun, seeing that Vasari, in the
second edition of his *Lives* (1568), speaks of it with unqualified admiration.
     Of the Virgins ascribed to Cimabue, the Uffizi's is the only certain one.
That in the Louvre, which comes from the church of San Francesco at Pisa,
is held by some to be slightly later. The one for Santa Maria dei Servi at
Bologna is today unanimously regarded as a shop product, while the one
from Santa Maria Novella, attributed to him by Vasari and now in the
Uffizi, is acknowledged by all to be the work of Duccio di Buoninsegna.
     The prophets at the bottom are: Jeremiah (on the scroll: Creavit
Dominus Novum super terram foemina circumdavit viro); Abraham (In
semine tuo benedicentur omnes gentes); David (De fructus ventris tui ponam
super sedem tuam); Isaiah (Ecce virgo concipivet et pariet).

GIOTTO (1267–1337)   *Florentine School*
THE MADONNA IN MAJESTY   Panel
Inv. No. 8344   Height 325 cm. (128″)
                                                 Width 204 cm. (80¹/₄″)

The altarpiece once stood on the altar of a chapel in San Salvatore in
Ognissanti, Florence, on the right of the door giving access to the choir.
This is attested by documents dating back to the first half of the fifteenth
century and confirmed by writers such as Ghiberti in his *Commentaries,*
the Anonimo Gaddiano in the *Codex Magliabecchiano,* now at the
Biblioteca Nazionale Centrale in Florence, and Vasari from the first
edition of his *Lives.*

The date now generally accepted is 1310—later, that is, than the
frescoes in the Scrovegni Chapel at Padua.

The novelty of this Madonna as compared with Cimabue's, which pre-
ceded it, lies above all in the composition. No longer are the figures of
the angels and saints just lined up about the Virgin's throne, but take
part, so to speak, in the action, forming an enraptured group as they
look upon the divine mother in silent ecstasy. This is the first image of
the Madonna to show her, not as the stern matron and queen of Byzantine
painting, but as the truly human virgin mother, foreshadowing the tender
intimacy of fifteenth-century representations. On the other hand, the artist
is still faithful to the grandeur of Italian Romanesque: in the sturdy
architecture of the throne; in the solidness of the powerful figure of the
Virgin, who reveals the Florentine forms of her body through the modelling
of the gown and mantle; and in the profound humanity of the Child,
already fully aware of His gesture of benediction. It is one of the most
forceful assertions of the master's feeling for plasticity (Toesca), in which
the colour accompanies the relief in a new way.

TADDEO GADDI (Died 1366)   *Florentine School*
THE MADONNA IN GLORY   Panel
Inv. Depositi No. 3   Height 154 cm. (60⅝")
                                                   Width   80 cm. (31½")

The picture is signed and dated 1355. From the church of San Pietro at Megognano near Poggibonsi it entered the Siena Gallery, and from there it went to Florence in 1914.

It is one of the two signed works by Taddeo Gaddi and is important for our knowledge of his late activity, of which it counts among the best products.

To the same period belongs the half-length *Virgin and Child* in the church of San Lorenzo alle Rose near Florence; it is less like the polyptych in San Giovanni Fuori Civitas at Pistoia, which dates from a few years earlier.

Here, as in all Taddeo's works, there is an obvious memory of Giotto, who had been his teacher. It is a memory that often conflicts with the Gothic elements penetrating into his art, which tended more and more towards a refined investigation of colour and decoration.

GIOTTINO (Mentioned 1324–1369)   *Florentine School*
THE DEPOSITION   Panel
Inv. No. 454   Height 184 cm. (72¹/₂")
                                         Width 134 cm. (52³/₄")

In his life of 'Tommaso called Giottino' (where he confuses the work
of two distinct artistic personalities), Vasari refers to this panel with the
highest praise. Today the picture is almost universally regarded as a work
by Giottino, to whom is also ascribed the tabernacles formerly in the
Via del Leone at Florence, and first in the Piazza di Santo Spirito, which
Vasari mentions too. There has been much discussion of the peculiarities
of the *Deposition,* in which elements have rightly been seen that break
away from the general tradition of fourteenth-century Florentine painting and suggest contacts with North Italian art—contacts, indeed, clearly
recognizable in other contemporary artists. But none of these elements can
cast doubts on the picture's undeniable Florentine origin within the
sphere of Giotto.

The most likely date is the second half of the fourteenth century—
though not very long after the middle and perhaps not later than 1370,
a date that accords, moreover, with the very scarce documentary references
to 'Giotto di maestro Stefano called Giottino'. For the grandeur of the
composition, for the vigour of the modelling, for the great refinement of
colouring that is nonetheless lively and bright, this picture counts among
the most remarkable proofs of the variety of aspects assumed by Florentine
painting after Giotto, despite its constant reassertions of its dependence
on him.

The picture was transferred to the Uffizi in 1842 from the church of
San Remigio at Florence.

SIMONE MARTINI (1284–1344) and
LIPPO MEMMI (Died 1357)   *Sienese School*
The Annunciation (in roundels at the sides, SS. Ansanus and
[?] Maxima)   Panel
Inv. Nos. 451, 452, 453   Height 265 cm. (104$^{1}/_{8}$″)
       Width 305 cm. (120$^{1}/_{8}$″)

The painting which is signed, was executed between 1329 and 1333 for
the Chapel of Sant' Ansano in Siena Cathedral. It actually bears the
date 1333, which is that of its completion. Towards the end of the
sixteenth century it was removed from the cathedral and taken to the
small church of Sant' Ansano at Castel Vecchio di Siena, under the
cathedral works department. From there it came in 1799 to the Uffizi in
exchange for two paintings by Luca Giordano. Unfortunately the original
frame was destroyed as early as the sixteenth century, when the picture's
shape was altered too, and the present frame is a nineteenth-century re-
construction. The *Annunciation* is one of the artist's greatest masterpieces.
With the inflexions of the line and the refinement of the colour he has
managed to express the feelings and stirrings of the soul, attaining to
stylistic heights never surpassed. The figures of the Virgin and the Angel
Gabriel provide a signal example of Gothic grace, which takes on a strong
musical quality in the balance of the composition, and they stand out
against the gold background with an almost incorporeal look that enhances
the religious significance of the scene. The saints in the top corners were
undoubtedly executed by Simone's brother-in-law Lippo Memmi, whose
name is inscribed on the painting, but this does not exclude the possibility
that at least their design goes back to Simone. Some have supposed that
other panels with figures of saints might exist, believing one of them to
have been identified in the *St John the Baptist* at Altenburg; but the perfect
unity of the work in its present form makes this hypothesis unlikely. Of
the two saints, the one on the left is St Ansanus, who was Siena's chief
protector, while the one on the right bears the name of St Julitta, who has
no connection with the city. On the other hand, St Maxima is associated
with both Siena and St Ansanus, with whom she was martyred, and her
name appears in descriptions of the picture dating back to the seventeenth
century.

PIETRO LORENZETTI (First half of fourteenth century)   *Sienese School*
THE MADONNA IN GLORY   Panel
Inv. No. 445   Height 145 cm. (57¹/₈″)
                                                       Width 122 cm. (48″)

The picture, signed and dated 1340, was painted for the church of San Francesco at Pistoia. It is already recorded by Vasari as 'an Our Lady, with some angels very well arranged about her'. He also speaks highly of the predella, now missing, where 'in a few scenes, he did some very small, very alert, very lively figures, which in those days was something wonderful'. The panel came to the Uffizi in 1799, made over by the Pistoian senator G. B. Cellesi in exchange for a Santi di Tito.

No doubt exists now about its date, which in the past was also read as 1315: the work fits perfectly into the development of Lorenzetti's art from the Arezzo polyptych of 1320, which still shows traces of the Assisi Giotto, to the grave and serene expression of the Siena *Birth of the Virgin,* done in 1342. The feeling for construction that Pietro acquired during these very years is here backed by the rich colouring, whose effect is decorative in spite of its essential sobriety. The motif of the 'silent colloquy of gazes that lovingly binds the mother to her child' is characteristic of the artist from the panel for Cortona Cathedral *(Virgin and Child with four Angels),* which is an early work; and its return in a picture like this, among the latest (Pietro is believed to have died during the plague of 1348), shows what a lasting effect on him was had by the work of Giovanni Pisano, from whom, indeed, Carli considers that he stems. Pietro's other work at the Uffizi, showing St Humility with scenes from her life, is almost contemporary with this.

LORENZO MONACO (First half of fifteenth century) *Florentine School*
THE ADORATION OF THE KINGS   Panel
Inv. No. 466   Height 144 cm. (56³/₄")
                                                      Width 177 cm. (69⁵/₈")

The painting went, as a Fra Angelico, from the friary of San Marco to the Accademia, and from there it came to the Uffizi in 1844. It is undated but probably belongs to a late phase of the artist's activity. Originally it was in the form of a triptych, and not until the end of the fifteenth century was it made rectangular, with the addition of the Annunciation figures and the prophets in the upper part, which are by Cosimo Rosselli, and with the almost complete abolition of the divisions between the original panels. The *Adoration* shows traces of the artist's work as an illuminator, which was predominant during his last years, and this is particularly apparent in the composition. In the colour, on the other hand, one observes a tendency towards warmer hues, which accounts for the former attribution of the painting to Fra Angelico. But Lorenzo Monaco is wholly Gothic, and is even the most notable representative of this period, which ended almost exactly in 1425, the year of his death. Nor should one forget the influence he had on various artists, especially through the activity of the school of illuminators that flourished chiefly with him in the Camaldolite monastery of Santa Maria degli Angeli. The *Adoration* certainly does not achieve the grandeur of the famous Uffizi *Coronation* or the nobility of some of the predella scenes from the same polyptych, but it is still delightful for the beauty of the faces and the characterization of each figure.

GENTILE DA FABRIANO (c. 1360– c. 1427)   *School of the Marches*
THE ADORATION OF THE MAGI   Panel
Inv. No. 8364   Height 300 cm. (118^1/$_8$")
                                            Width 282 cm. (111")

Painted for the Palla Strozzi chapel in the sacristy of Santa Trinità at
Florence, the work is signed and dated 1423. Vasari says the artist 'did
a life-like portrait of himself': it is probably the figure seen full-face in
a dark red cap behind the standing king. This very famous picture had
enormous influence on fifteenth-century Florentine art, attracting the
attention and arousing the admiration of Masaccio himself, as Giovanni
Poggi has shown. Fra Filippo Lippi took from it compositional elements
and illustratory details for his tondo with the *Adoration of the Kings*,
now at Washington. Gentile, who came from the North, has exemplified in
his *Adoration* the style known as International Gothic, which held sway
in Europe at that time. But he achieved an unusual richness of composition
and a really warm charm in the faces, through the lively colours, the
refined decorations, and a passionate love of nature, which led him to
adorn the frame with realistically painted floral motifs and to devise
imaginative landscapes in which one again finds details of this style; yet
already during his stay at Florence, to which his best works belong, he
gave proof of an originality in which there reappeared elements of what
he had learned in his earliest training. This *Adoration* remains an
enchanting example of an art that in Italy was soon to be overwhelmed
by the new Florentine School of Masaccio and his followers. Of the
predella, on which Gentile also lavished the grace of his fanciful dream
forms, only two panels are still in Florence: the *Nativity* and the *Flight
into Egypt*. The third, with the *Presentation in the Temple*, is at the
Louvre.

MASACCIO *(Tommaso Guidi)* (1401–1428)   *Florentine School*
THE VIRGIN AND CHILD WITH ST ANNE   Panel
Inv. No. 8386   Height 175 cm. (68⁷/₈″)
          Width 103 cm. (40¹/₂″)

Vasari, in the second edition of his *Lives* (1568), records this picture as
being in the church of Sant' Ambrogio at Florence. Some have assumed
it to be the middle part of a triptych, but Vasari's reference only concerns
the panel as it appears today. In any case it is without doubt an early
work datable around 1420, partly because of the connections with
Masolino. Already noted by the critics, these have been confirmed by the
recent restoration, which has freed the panel from areas of repaint added
to hide a careless eighteenth-century restoration. The point has thus been
reached of distinguishing the particular parts attributable to each artist.
But considering the work's unquestionable unity of composition and
some definitely Masaccesque traits even in the figures claimed to be by
Masolino, it seems more advisable to regard the work as being in substance
by Masaccio, and to limit Masolino's share to that of an assistant, who
in this case is actually supposed to have been the master. It is obvious
that the painting is essentially fifteenth century and therefore already an
embodiment of those ideas and visions that Masaccio may have learnt from
Donatello and Brunelleschi. The central group, which is certainly
Masaccesque in its spatial perspective and in the plasticity of the figures
brought about by the light, has a characteristic stamp that can be associated
only with the painter of certain scenes in the Brancacci Chapel. And
the capital letters of the inscription have rightly been considered, like the
Child's nakedness, a fifteenth-century innovation.

FRA ANGELICO (Fra Giovanni da Fiesole) (c. 1400–1455)

Florentine School

THE CORONATION OF THE VIRGIN

Inv. No. 1612

Panel

Height 112 cm. (44⁷/₈")

Width 114 cm. (44¹/₂")

Vasari, and before him Antonio Manetti and other writers, saw this picture on the choir-screen in Santa Maria Nuova, also called Sant' Egidio, the church of the Florentine hospital. It came to the Uffizi from the hospital in 1825. Most critics place the picture round about 1425, though some date it 1430–40. If it really is a reduction to a smaller scale of the *Coronation* painted for San Domenico at Fiesole and now in the Louvre, then one would have to date it to after 1440. But its connection with the Louvre picture is not such as to justify this hypothesis, for it actually includes very different elements, all of which are entirely referable to Fra Angelico, particularly in the composition and the luminosity of the colour. Hence the recent attribution to Fra Angelico's co-worker Zanobi Strozzi must also be rejected; if one is willing to grant that some collaboration did occur, this was not of a sort that prevents the painting from being rightfully included in the catalogue of Fra Angelico's works. The best idea, therefore, is to choose a date within the limits of those mentioned above, and preferably to go back to about 1435. Another reason for this dating is the maturity shown in the picture as compared with those that are definitely earlier. It is not absolutely certain that the work had a predella, to which the two small panels at the Museo di San Marco with the Marriage and Burial of the Virgin are supposed to have belonged. Nevertheless, one must acknowledge that these come very close to the *Coronation* in style and are, therefore, to be placed in the same years. But their different fate—they entered the Medici collections as early as the seventeenth century—and the silence of the early sources make it doubtful whether they really are connected with the *Coronation*. This has always been a very famous picture, and its reputation is justified by the fact that it presents one of the most essential and original aspects of Fra Angelico's painting: the intense mysticism of his youthful period and that which directly followed.

98

PAOLO UCCELLO (c. 1396–1475)   *Florentine School*
THE BATTLE OF SAN ROMANO   Panel
Inv. No. 479   Height 182 cm. (71⁵/₈″)
Width 323 cm. (127¹/₂″)

The picture comes from the Palazzo Medici in the Via Larga. According
to the inventory of the works left by Lorenzo the Magnificent, it was in
the big ground-floor room along with two others illustrating the same
battle, a fourth showing combats of dragons and lions, a fifth with the
story of Paris—all these by Paolo Uccello—and a hunting scene by
Francesco Pesello. The other two pictures of the Battle of San Romano
are at the Louvre and the National Gallery, London. That of the Uffizi
was in the middle, and it is signed. The battle celebrated here was won by
the Florentines on 1 June 1432 against Siena and the Visconti. They
were under the command of Niccolò da Tolentino, to whom the equestrian
picture frescoed in Florence Cathedral by Andrea del Castagno was
dedicated in 1456. Without any doubt at all, these are among the artist's
greatest masterpieces. He has given free rein to his imagination, fixing on
the canvas the tangle of the combatants. This affords him an occasion for
making ever new experiments with perspective, though without forgoing
a balance of masses that reveals his remarkable skill in composition. The
colour is kept to an almost uniform tone and has darkened a bit with
time; but in the horses of the foreground appear broad areas of hues at
once lively and fanciful, which constitute the picture's most individual
charm, together with the prodigious variety and even grotesqueness of the
attitudes. Certainly, no other work of art could have formed a better
adornment for the room of that cultured gentleman and able politician,
Lorenzo the Magnificent; but the painter must have received the commission from Cosimo the Elder himself, who was still alive at that date.

ALESSO BALDOVINETTI (1425?–1499) *Florentine School*
The Madonna and Child with Saints Panel
Inv. No. 487 Height 174 cm. (68¹/₂")
Width 166 cm. (65³/₈")

Painted for the chapel of the Villa Medici at Cafaggiolo, this work came
to the Uffizi in 1796. It must have been executed round about 1454, when
Alesso was no longer in the studio of Domenico Veneziano, with whom
he had worked on the frescoes in Sant' Egidio; but it is still an early
production. The villa at Cafaggiolo had been rebuilt for Cosimo by
Michelozzo. Formerly identified as St Vitalis, the holy armed knight must
in fact be St Julian, who together with his neighbour St Lawrence serves
to recall Cosimo's nephews Lorenzo, later known as the Magificent, and
his brother Giuliano. They are matched on the other side by the two
doctor saints who protected the family, Cosmas and Damian. It has also
been conjectured that the picture may have been commissioned in 1453
by Piero the Gouty on the occasion of the birth of his second son Giuliano,
partly because this would account for the adding of St Peter to the other
saints already connected with the family. Actually, there is corroboration
for either date in the artist's style, which shows the influence of Andrea
del Castagno as well as Fra Angelico and Domenico Veneziano. Notable
is the pose of the Child lying on His mother's knees, a motif new to the
Florentine painting of those years, like the presence of an Anatolian rather
than a Persian or Sicilian carpet, as Ruth Wedgwood Kennedy has
observed. But what the artist borrowed from his masters, whether in the
composition, which has precedents in Fra Angelico, or in the forms,
which derive chiefly from Andrea, he has transmuted into something
personal, infusing a delicacy and a gaiety typical of his best pictures.

FRA FILIPPO LIPPI (c. 1406–1469)   *Florentine School*
THE MADONNA AND CHILD WITH SCENES FROM THE LIFE
OF THE VIRGIN   Panel
Inv. Palatina No. 343   Diam. 135 cm. (53¹/₈″)

In a Prato document of 1452, reference is made to a tondo with a story
of the Virgin Mary that Fra Filippo had begun painting for Leonardo di
Bartolommeo Bartolini, a citizen of Florence. It is thought that this tondo
may be the one now at the Pitti, though when and how the latter
entered the Medici collections is not known. Acceptance of the hypothesis
is hindered by the fact that on the back of the panel has been drawn a
very beautiful escutcheon with a griffin rampant, which does not
correspond to the bearing of the Bartolini family of Florence. It should
be noted, on the other hand, that the style of both the painting and the
drawing suits the date 1452, which is when the frescoes for Prato Cathedral
were begun.

 This is a work in which the artist asserted his own personality and
liberated himself from the Fra Angelico influence that had dominated
him before. He has composed the scene freely, aiming above all at giving
life to it with the smaller ones of the Virgin's birth and the meeting
between Joachim and St Anne at the Golden Gate, which thus contribute
to that humanization of the holy scene which is a feature of nearly all
his religious paintings. But it is primarily in the figure of the Virgin that
this humanization becomes increasingly apparent, yet without detracting
from the image's sacred character which is entrusted to the purity of the
face and the gentleness it radiates. Lippi had previously done another
tondo, which is now at the National Gallery of Art, Washington, and
shows the *Adoration of the Magi.* There he kept to a composition with
superimposed layers, as a support for the round shape. But in the Pitti
tondo, having to depict a less complex scene, he inscribed the main group
and the collateral episodes perfectly in the circle, giving us one of Italian
painting's most successful and coherent representations.

PIERO DELLA FRANCESCA (Died 1492)   *Florentine School*
PORTRAITS OF FEDERICO DA MONTEFELTRO, DUKE OF URBINO, AND HIS WIFE
BATTISTA SFORZA (on the backs, two allegorical compositions)
Inv. No. 1615   Panel
Height 47 cm. (18½″)
Width 33 cm. (13″)

These two portraits came to Florence with the Della Rovere collections, which were inherited in 1631 by Vittoria della Rovere, then Grand Duchess of Tuscany through her marriage to Ferdinando II de' Medici. They entered the Uffizi in 1773. Until recently they were believed to have been painted in 1465 or 1466, owing to the date of the testimony of a Veronese humanist, who mentions a portrait of Federico done by Piero. Lionello Venturi has rightly remarked, however, that the inscription referring to Battista on the back of her portrait is in the past tense. It must therefore be taken that the entire work was produced after 1473, the year of Battista's death, and not just her own portrait, since the diptych was conceived as a whole, as the background landscapes show. Moreover, it had already been pointed out that Battista's features here are those of a woman more advanced in years than she was in 1466. Federico has the countenance of a man used to bearing arms, at once bold and wary, but not without an expression that is well suited to the other facet of his personality: that of a generous patron of the arts and literature. Battista is calm but severe, despite the splendour of her gown, her jewels, and her head-dress. That simplicity with which Piero rendered his figures in the frescoes at San Francesco, Arezzo, returns in these two portraits, where fidelity to the model is transfigured by the geometrical structure of the forms and by the transparency and luminosity of the atmosphere.

On the backs of the portraits have been depicted the Triumphs of the Duke and his consort. Federico is accompanied by the four cardinal virtues: Justice, Prudence, Temperance, and Fortitude; Battista by the three theological virtues: Faith, Hope and Charity. Crowned by Fame, Federico is seated on a triumphal car drawn by two white horses under the control of an amorino. Battista is reading as she sits on her car, drawn by a pair of unicorns whose driver is again an amorino. Below there are the two inscriptions done in very beautiful capitals, one extolling Federico's glory and success, the other Battista's goodness. The usual arrangement of such Triumphs has here been transformed by the landscape, which is not, as in the portraits, a fanciful background, but an inseparable part of the very place where the scene unfolds.

107

ANTONIO DEL POLLAIUOLO (1429–1498) *Florentine School*
PORTRAIT OF A WOMAN SEEN IN PROFILE Panel
Inv. No. 1491 Height 55 cm. (21⁵/₈″)
Width 34.5 cm. (13⁵/₈″)

The painting came from the Palazzo Pitti in 1861. It was attributed to
Piero della Francesca, but the many retouchings prevented mention of the
name that even then seemed the most appropriate: Antonio del Pollaiuolo.
Today, restored as far as possible to its original condition, the portrait
leaves no doubt that it comes from Antonio's hand and must therefore
join the other two previously more famous ones: that of the Museo Poldi-
Pezzoli at Milan, which was also once ascribed to Piero della Francesca,
and that of the Berlin Museum which represents the same woman
slightly younger and used to be attributed to Domenico Veneziano. The
Uffizi portrait is even more Pollaiuolesque in the face, in the hardness of
the contours, in the lighting of the hair, in the highly successful rendering
of the details of dress and necklace, and it takes its place in the series of
female profiles from the Florentine fifteenth century that are so distinctive
in the way they stand out against the light background of the sky.

SANDRO BOTTICELLI (1444/5--1510)   *Florentine School*
THE RETURN OF JUDITH   Panel
Inv. No. 1484   Height 31 cm. (12$^1/_8$")
                 Width 24 cm.   (9$^1/_2$")

Raffaele Borghini, a continuator of Vasari in the art-historical literature of the sixteenth century, tells us in his *Riposo* (1584) that this little
panel, together with the small picture representing the tent of Holofernes,
belonged to the sculptor Rodolfo Sirigatti, who presented them both to
Bianca Capello, the second wife of Grand Duke Francesco de' Medici.
As a legacy from her son Don Antonio de' Medici, Prince of Capistrano,
the two works entered the grand-ducal collection in 1632. They formed
a diptych and are universally considered to date from the artist's early
period, round about 1470, when he already knew how to add dramatic
force to the gracefulness of his figures and the refinement of his colours.
In the panel that shows Judith followed by a maid-servant carrying the
head of Holofernes in a basket, one is struck above all by the elegance
of Judith in her light, fluttering dress that contrasts with the heavy garment
of the maid. Here the artist is under the influence of Antonio del Pollaiuolo
and his dynamic line. It is an influence that will persist for a long time
and often appear in his work, even through the colouring with its bolder
hues. But also in this picture the influence of Fra Filippo Lippi can still
be seen through the transformation of the realism and dramatic sense of
his frescoes at Prato.

A replica of the painting, once in the palace of the Prince of Fondi at
Naples, was at first ascribed to Filippino Lippi. Having come into the
possession of the antiquary Stefano Bardini who reassigned it to Botticelli,
it thereafter passed through various hands, attributed to the school of
Botticelli and then again to Filippino. Now it is in the Cincinnati Art
Museum as a Botticelli.

SANDRO BOTTICELLI (1444/5–1510)   *Florentine School*
PORTRAIT OF A MAN WITH A MEDAL   Panel
Inv. No. 1488   Height 57.5 cm. (22⁵/₈″)
                                         Width 44 cm. (17³/₈″)

This picture comes from the collection left by Cardinal Carlo de' Medici
in 1666. The medal that the man holds in his hands is Florentine work
and dates back to between 1465 and 1470, as it bears the title *Pater
Patriae*, which was conferred on Cosimo the Elder in 1465, and is reproduced in an illuminated codex done for Piero de' Medici, who died
in 1469. At one time it was attributed to Andrea del Castagno and was
believed to represent Giovanni Pico della Mirandola. After it had been
recognized as the work of Botticelli, varied attempts were made to identify the sitter. Having rejected Cosimo the Elder's son Piero the Gouty
because he was far more mature at this period, and also his other son
Giovanni, already dead in 1461, people have thought he might be the
unknown artist who designed the medal or else someone to whom the
Medici had presented it for special services. Greatly superior to Botticelli's
other early portraits through its assurance of structure and expression,
through the effort to render the sitter's intense vitality, this one reveals
the influence of both Alesso Baldovinetti and Pollaiuolo in the chiaroscuro
modelling of the hands, in the streaking of clouds in the sky, in the
landscape, and in every other element of the linear design.

SANDRO BOTTICELLI (1444/5–1510)　　　　*Florentine School*
ALLEGORY OF SPRING (La Primavera)　　　　　　Panel
Inv. No. 8360　　　　　　　　　　Height 203 cm. (79⁷/₈″)
　　　　　　　　　　　　　　　　Width 314 cm. (123⁵/₈″)

This picture was painted for the Villa of Castello, near Florence, which belonged to Lorenzo di Pierfrancesco de' Medici, a great-nephew of Cosimo the Elder. It was seen there by Vasari when the villa had become the property of Duke Cosimo I. Afterwards it entered the grand-ducal repository, from which it came to the Uffizi during the nineteenth century. Attempts have been made to connect the *Primavera* with Poliziano's *Stanze per la Giostra* for the joust in which Giuliano de' Medici, the brother of Lorenzo the Magnificent, took part; but it seems near the mark to see in the painting the inspiration of either the poems written by Lorenzo himself or the teaching of Poliziano, who used to lecture at the Studio Fiorentino on the classical texts of Ovid, Horace and Lucretius, and who in certain of his minor compositions offers some real points of correspondence with the figures in the picture. According to the latest studies, a more direct source of this allegory is to be found in Apuleius and the image symbolizes Venus-Humanitas, which also accords with a passage in Marsilio Ficino.

　In the middle of the garden that provides the setting, we see Venus Genetrix. Above her Cupid shoots an arrow, and to the left the Graces perform a dance. On the right Zephyrus, a winged youth with his hair and cloak agitated by the wind, is in the act of grasping a fleeing girl, the nymph Chloris, over whom he sends a vigorous puff. From her mouth she casts flowers that fall into the lap of Spring, who, wearing a dress adorned with flowers, scatters on the ground all those she has collected. On the other side Mercury is dispersing the mists with his wand. Because of the links with Poliziano mentioned above, the painting, which is somewhat darkened by old varnish, must date from about 1480: certainly from after 1477, the year when the guardians of Pierfrancesco's sons acquired the property on which the Villa of Castello was built, and from before Botticelli's departure for Rome. It is therefore the first work of the artist's maturity to show all his creative power and his poetic interpretation of the classical world. In the naturalistic accuracy with which the grass is represented one can also see Leonardo's influence. But the frontal composition, which moreover has its origins in the antique style, derives rather from Antonio del Pollaiuolo towards whose art Botticelli increasingly tended.

SANDRO BOTTICELLI (1444/5–1510) 	*Florentine School*
THE BIRTH OF VENUS 	Canvas
Inv. No. 878 	Height 175 cm. (68⁷/₈")
	Width 278.5 cm. (109¹/₂")

This picture was painted for the Villa of Castello, near Florence, which belonged to Lorenzo di Pierfrancesco de' Medici, a great-nephew of Cosimo the Elder. Vasari saw it there, after the villa had become the possession of Duke Cosimo I, the heir to that branch of the Medici family: 'Venus being born, and those breezes and winds that waft her to shore with the Cupids'. As in the case of the *Allegory of Spring,* one can only say that the work was partly inspired by Poliziano's *Stanze.* Standing on a shell, the goddess moves towards the shore, where she is received by a nymph in a dress adorned with cornflowers and roses, who throws her a cloak which is also decorated with flowers. This nymph may be intended to represent Spring, and she is balanced on the left by Zephyrus and Chloris, who fly along pushing the goddess with their breath. The goddess's figure brings to mind the classical statues of Venus Anadyomene, but it has an entirely new feeling, in the rosy brightness of the limbs, the waviness of the hair, and the elegance of the slightly undulant movement. This really is Botticelli's masterpiece, thanks to the intensity of poetic expression achieved through the harmony of the composition, the gracefulness of the movement, and the general lightness of the colour. The work must date back to the years following his return from Rome, round about 1485; and it is certainly the one that reflects best the humanist circle in which he developed and which enhances most the merits of Florentine drawing, which he had studied in the great artists of his period ever since he had begun to paint. It is thus the work that reveals his style most fully and throws light in particular on the essentially spiritual character even of his profane images, which are always fanciful but always governed in their action by a perfect measure, unsurpassable and unsurpassed, which gives them universal and eternal value.

116

SANDRO BOTTICELLI (1444/5–1510)   *Florentine School*
THE ADORATION OF THE MAGI   Panel
Inv. No. 882   Height 111 cm. (43³/₄″)
                                                       Width 134 cm. (52³/₄″)

The picture was painted for an altar of the Lama family in the church
of Santa Maria Novella, Florence, where Vasari saw it on the front wall
to the left of the main door. Probably removed from this site when an
altar was built there in the sixteenth century for another family, it then
became the property of Don Fabio Mondragone, a nobleman at the Medici
court; but we do not know when it entered the grand-ducal collections.
It came to the Uffizi from the Villa del Poggio Imperiale in 1796. The
picture's fame is partly due to the fact that Botticelli has given his figures
the features of some of the Medici family. The three kings resemble Cosimo
the Elder, Piero di Cosimo, called the Gouty, and Giovanni di Cosimo.
Giuliano di Piero, killed in the Pazzi Conspiracy, is recognizable in the
black-haired young man on the right, bowing his head, and Lorenzo the
Magnificent in the bare-headed one on the left, with a sword. The
figure looking out at the spectator, on the far right, is probably a self-
portrait of Botticelli. This picture seems to belong to the painter's maturity—round about 1475 rather than ten years later, as some have supposed,
both because it already reflects the firm orientation towards Pollaiuolo
that was completed at this time, and because one can perhaps discern traces
of Filippino Lippi, who had entered Botticelli's workshop by 1472. The
noble dignity of the way the scene has been composed greatly excels that
found in the previous *Adoration,* a tondo at the National Gallery, London:
the central group is more monumental, the execution very refined, and the
faces have been rendered with wonderful power. All the figures probably
represent members of the Medici court, though in many cases it would
not be easy to establish their exact identity. Thus, besides its value as a
religious image, this picture also serves a social and commemorative
purpose, which transcends the purely humanistic factors, even though
these are important.

SANDRO BOTTICELLI (1444/5–1510)　　　*Florentine School*
PALLAS AND THE CENTAUR　　　　　　　　　　　Canvas
Inv. Depositi No. 29　　　　　　　　　Height 207 cm. (81½″)
　　　　　　　　　　　　　　　　　　　Width 148 cm. (58¼″)

Like the *Allegory of Spring* and the *Birth of Venus*, this picture was
painted for Lorenzo di Pierfrancesco de' Medici's Villa of Castello. It
must belong to the period immediately after Botticelli's return from Rome.
Some have tried to see in the picture the apotheosis of Lorenzo the
Magnificent, who, after the successful negotiations with the King of
Naples, quelled violence and opened an era of peace; but it can be more
easily interpreted, on a humanist plane, as Wisdom conquering Ignorance.
Besides, such an allegory is thoroughly in keeping with the purchaser,
whom we know to have been among Marsilio Ficino's favourite pupils,
and also with Lorenzo the Magnificent (who perhaps had been involved in
the tutelage of the young Lorenzo). More than the other mythological
allegories painted for the villa, this one shows a direct connection with
antique representations in the plasticity of the figures and in the closer ad-
herence to the types and proportions usual in classical art – possibly as a
result of what Botticelli had been able to see during his stay at Rome.
Yet here again it is not a question of simple borrowings from antiquity
but of original restatements by the artist. In the rhythm of the figures and
the fluidity of the contours he has sought to produce images that are
definite and clearly established yet still belong completely to his own
special figurative world. This *Pallas* cannot be identified with the one
Vasari mentions as being 'over a device of indentations emitting fire',
or with the one on the standard that Giuliano de' Medici bore at the
joust in 1475, also painted by Botticelli. Neither of these has survived.

120

SANDRO BOTTICELLI (1444/5–1510) *Florentine School*
CALUMNY Panel
Inv. No. 1496 Height 62.5 cm. (24⅝")
Width 91.5 cm. (36")

According to Vasari, Botticelli gave this picture to his very close friend
Antonio Segni, who was also a friend of Leonardo's. In Vasari's day it
was at the home of a cultured descendant of Segni, called Fabio. We do
not know when it entered the grand-ducal collections, but it came to the
Uffizi from the private archives at the Palazzo Pitti in 1773. The artist
has followed the description Leon Battista Alberti gives in his treatise
Della Pittura of the painting by Apelles, as Lucian of Samosata represents
it in one of his dialogues. The judge is enthroned on the right, between
Suspicion and Ignorance. Before him Spite (or Envy) is leading a young
woman—Calumny—who drags naked Innocence along, while Duplicity
and Deceit adorn her. On the left Penitence looks grimly at Truth. The
action unfolds in a sumptuous marble arcade, with statues in the niches
and gilded reliefs on the friezes and vaults. Renaissance artists loved these
reconstructions of ancient pictures, and especially of Apelles' *Calumny*.
This is the oldest surviving example and undoubtedly the most beautiful,
thanks to the original way of interpreting antiquity that is characteristic
of Botticelli and leads him to include Renaissance ornaments and statues
of a fifteenth-century type in the deliberately antique-style architecture—
ornaments and statues that often have some link with justice. Here he has
attained a loftiness of inspiration, a clearness of representation, and a
nobility and elegance of composition that make this picture the masterpiece of his late period. On the same level are the effectiveness of the
dramatic expression and vigour of the movement, which accompany an
unsurpassed refinement in the execution. Even if stylistically it ought
not to date from later than 1495, the picture belongs to the group of
work which also have a clear moral purpose, corresponding to the spiritual crisis, perhaps brought about by Savonarola, that Botticelli too suffered during these years.

DOMENICO GHIRLANDAIO (1449–1494)   *Florentine School*
THE VIRGIN ENTHRONED BETWEEN SS DIONYSIUS
THE AREOPAGITE, DOMINIC, CLEMENT I, AND THOMAS
AQUINAS   Panel
Inv. No. 8388   Height 168 cm. (66^1/$_8$″)
                                   Width 197 cm. (77^5/$_8$″)

This panel no doubt came from a Dominican house, in view of the presence of St Thomas Aquinas and St Dominic. It probably belongs to the
penultimate decade of the century, between the frescoes Ghirlandaio
painted at Rome in the Sistine Chapel and those at Florence that constitute
his most mature (in the Sassetti Chapel of Santa Trinità) or his most
famous work (as in the apse of Santa Maria Novella). The picture still
bears traces of what had been the artist's best introduction in the exquisite sweetness of the central group, where the motif of the Virgin with
her Child echoes that in the panel painted for the Jesuit college at Florence (now also in the Uffizi), which is among his earliest and most
successful works. If anything, one is conscious of the inspiration being
less spontaneous now in the basic composition as also in the impressive
and statuesque images of St Dionysius and St Clement. Indeed, the types
of the figures and draperies will often reappear in his altarpieces. Here,
the background is more completely architectural than in the Jesuit picture.
Trees rise up behind the marble-panelled reredos, on which stand vases
of flowers, while the lilies in the vases held by the angels on each side
of the throne form with their extremely long stems a motif adding
splendour to the whole.

There is a predella with the *Entombment* at the centre between four
scenes from the life of the saints in the main panel. Today the prevailing
view is that this predella was painted chiefly by one of Ghirlandaio's best
assistants, Bartolommeo di Giovanni.

LUCA SIGNORELLI (c. 1445/50–1523)   *Tuscan School*
THE HOLY FAMILY WITH A FEMALE SAINT
Inv. Palatina 355   Diam: 99 cm. (39″)

This painting has been identified, in all probability, with a painting by Signorelli quoted in a seventeenth-century catalogue; in which case it would have been sent from Florence to Siena 'for the service of the Most Serene Prince Mattias de' Medici' (Mattias, son of Cosimo II, lived from 1613 to 1667 and was Governor of Siena three times).

We do not know just when the painting became part of the Medici collections. It is undoubtedly a work by Signorelli, despite the fact that Adolfo Venturi in 1915 and Dussler have sought to see in it the work of a pupil. We are persuaded by the originality of the composition which has disposed the figures to follow the shape of the frame and accentuate the main subject of the scene, which is the conversation between the Virgin and the saint who sits writing. In all this we can also see a reflection of the Florentine experience of the artist, who, having travelled many times to Florence in the last decades of the fifteenth century, would certainly have come under the influence of that atmosphere. The sweetness and beauty of expression in the Mother and Son have been brought out, as also the intensity of expression in the posture of the saint. The breadth of style, the movement and life animating the faces, have lost some of their impact due to the blackening of colour as a result of clumsy restoring.

There have been varying opinions from critics as to the dating of the painting: Venturi and Dussler, as also Mancini and Ciaranfi, all consider it to be a late work of the master. Berenson and Cruttwell, however, include it among his earlier works. Salmi considers it not much earlier than the last decade of the fifteenth century, and this opinion is born out by the signs heralding a sixteenth-century taste, such as the greater complexity of the composition and the larger proportions of the faces.

PIETRO PERUGINO (1446–1523)   *Umbrian School*
THE MADONNA AND CHILD WITH THE
INFANT ST JOHN AND AN ANGEL   Panel
Inv. Palatina No. 219   Height 88 cm. (34⁵/₈″)
                                                Width 86 cm. (33⁷/₈″)

The picture came as a Perugino with the legacy of Cardinal Leopoldo de' Medici. It is a variant of the central panel of the altarpiece Perugino did for the Certosa near Pavia, parts of which are now at the National Gallery, London. The Pitti version has been modified by adding the infant St John and reducing the height (so that the three angels singing in the sky, which were done by an assistant anyway, are excluded), but it is certainly authentic in all essentials. Since the Certosa altarpiece can be placed round about 1500, the work under consideration was presumably at a date not far from this, as indeed an examination of its style confirms. The composition also reappears in a tondo from Perugino's workshop (now at the Liechtenstein Galerie, Vienna), where the Virgin kneeling in prayer before the Child, who is supported on a sack by an angel, stands out against a landscape background in which shepherds are dancing on the right. This landscape has more of Raphael than Perugino about it, according to Cavalcaselle, and is less precisely executed. The different shape and the absence of details certainly owed to assistants could also lead one to think that the Pitti version represents the artist's first idea for the composition; and to support this theory there is the beauty of the landscape, the expressive calmness of the Virgin's face, the delicacy of the colour, and above all the greater intensity of feeling, even in comparison with the London version. Berenson too agrees that at least most of the picture is authentic. We do not know from whom Cardinal Leopoldo acquired the painting.

FRANCESCO FRANCIA (1450?–1517) 　　　　*Bolognese School*
PORTRAIT OF EVANGELISTA SCAPPI 　　　　　　　　　Panel
Inv. No. 1444 　　　　　　　　　　　Height 55 cm. (21⅝")
　　　　　　　　　　　　　　　　　Width 44.5 cm. (17½")

The identification of the figure is based on the writing in the letter he
holds in his right hand. He is a member of the Bolognese Scappi family,
which had dealings with Francia and still owned works by him in the
following century. It was Francia, in fact, who painted the altarpiece
commissioned by Giovanni Scappi for the family chapel in the church
of Santa Maria dei Servi. This work, which shows the Virgin and Child
with the infant St John and SS. Paul and Francis, is now in the Pinacoteca
at Bologna. The portrait must date from the first decade of the sixteenth
century, and it actually still contains some of those echoes of Perugino
that are even more common in the artist's early works. The type accords
with the other portraits by Francia, in the figure's tranquil nature, the
gentle expression, the firmly closed mouth, the exact rendering of the
attire, and the action of holding a book or paper. Though the Uffizi shows
greater freedom and softness in the skilful modelling of the face, there
is still the same yearning for an ideal of delicate, pensive beauty, which
also prevails in his religious scenes and even gets reflected in the landscapes
that form a background to the figures.

The painting came to the Uffizi from the Palazzo Pitti in 1773.

GIOVANNI BELLINI (1428–1516)   *Venetian School*
SACRED ALLEGORY   Panel
Inv. No. 903   Height 73 cm. (28³/₄″)
                                        Width 119 cm. (46⁷/₈″)

The work came from the Imperial Gallery at Vienna in 1793 as part of
a profitable exchange for pictures from the Florentine gallery. This exchange was promoted by Luigi Lanzi, then the royal antiquary, and it
included masterpieces by Titian, Palma, and Dürer. At that time the painting was considered a Bellini, but in 1825 it was attributed to Giorgione,
and later to Marco Basaiti. The authorship was eventually restored to
Bellini by Giovanni Morelli. The scene depicted here has been the subject
of several different readings, owing to its plainly allegorical character. One
connects it with a French poem of the fourteenth century by Guillaume
de Deguileville, *Le Pèlerinage de l'âme,* according to which it would
represent the Garden of Paradise, where the souls from Purgatory (the
innocent children) pause before the Madonna and various saints. Even
this interpretation has lately been contested and replaced by the generic
one of *Sacra Conversazione.* Anyway, the artist has created for this scene
a marvellous landscape with a harmony of hues blending in the luminous
atmosphere, motifs rendered in strict perspective, and subtleties of execution that herald Giorgione's conquests. Wrapped in a vast stillness, the
participants in the sacred allegory gather on the many coloured marble
terrace opening towards the sheet of water.
    It is generally thought that this picture should be placed round about
1490—that is, during the best period of the artist's activity, when his
masterpieces appeared in quick succession, from the altarpiece for the
church of San Pietro Martire in Murano to the Berlin *Resurrection* and
the Naples *Transfiguration.* The perfect unity of the composition over-
comes the obscurity in the representation of the subject, as the setting is
such an integral part of the image, in which the loving care bestowed on
the form is matched by the masterliness of the colour, with its very
delicate transitions and enamel-like brilliance.

ANDREA MANTEGNA (1431–1506)   *Veneto School*
THE ADORATION OF THE KINGS,
(Wings: The Circumcision, and the Ascension)   Panel
Inv. No. 910
                              Central Panel: Height 77 cm. (30¼")
                                                 Width 75 cm. (29½")

In his life of Andrea Mantegna, Vasari mentions 'a small panel painting
in which there are scenes with figures that are not very big but extremely
beautiful', which the marquis Lodovico Gonzaga had had the artist
execute for the chapel of the Castello at Mantua. According to P.
Kristeller and later critics this is to be recognized in the work now at
the Uffizi. But such an identification conflicts with the fact that the
chapel seems still to have contained some pictures by Mantegna in 1457–
this on the authority of a writer who only offers hearsay evidence—
whereas the Uffizi paintings already belonged to the Grand Duke of
Tuscany by that date. Fiocco therefore thought that the Uffizi panels
might have been commissioned from the artist when he was staying at
Florence in 1466–67 by some member of the Medici family. However,
during the recent Mantegna exhibition at Mantua (1961), it was established
that the small panel with the *Death of the Virgin* at the Prado, completed,
according to Longhi, by the fragment in a private collection at Ferrara,
would acquire the dimensions of the Florentine panels, thus confirming
Longhi's theory that it belongs to the same ensemble. Whether the latter
really should be connected with the chapel of the Castello or with another work by the artist is thus still uncertain. In any case, the Uffizi
panels are undoubtedly of the highest quality, through the grandeur of
the compositions, the monumentality of the figures, the fresh interpretation
of classical architecture, the richness of the decoration, and the enamel-
like colours that clothe the rigidly sculptural forms. Mantegna has here
achieved a style of his own in which he has absorbed Tuscan influences,
from Andrea del Castagno to Donatello, in a novel way, though without
forgetting his Veneto origins, as the landscapes show.

   It is not known what adventures befell the three panels on their way
to Don Antonio de' Medici, who already owned them in 1587 and who
left them, when he died in 1632, to Grand Duke Ferdinando II. They
were separate then and even had different attributions; the *Adoration*
being considered a Botticelli. Not until the end of the eighteenth century
did they regain a common attribution, and at the beginning of the nineteenth they were arbitrarily combined as a triptych.

ANDREA DEL VERROCCHIO (1435–1488)   *Florentine School*
THE BAPTISM OF CHRIST   Panel
Inv. No. 8358   Height 177 cm. (69⁵/₈")
                                                       Width 151 cm. (59¹/₂")

This painting was executed for the monastery church of San Salvi on the
outskirts of Florence. It then passed, after the siege of 1530, which
almost destroyed this monastery, into the other Vallombrosan house of
Santa Verdiana; from there it came to the Accademia, and in 1919 to
the Uffizi. There is an old tradition, attested as early at 1510, that the
angel on the spectator's left was done by Leonardo da Vinci, when, as
a pupil of Verrocchio's, he helped him paint this picture; and that the
master, seeing himself thus excelled, did not want to touch a brush again.
It is a fact that this angel already contains the seeds of all Leonardo's
painting. The picture dates from shortly after 1470, and Leonardo's
intervention through the angel, from before 1475. Today it is almost
universally considered that the painting was not finished straight away
and that Leonardo worked on it later too: in the landscape, which does
indeed foreshadow the Leonardesque landscape, and perhaps in the figure
of Christ as well. On the other hand the composition is undoubtedly
Verrocchio's, and one sees its influence in works by other pupils, such
as Lorenzo di Credi. To Verrocchio must certainly also be ascribed the
Baptist, on account of the modelling, the sharpness of the contours, the
completely plastic form, which is well suited to an artist who was prin-
cipally a sculptor; and the second angel, whose more obvious humanity
and lower spiritual plane make it very different from the Leonardesque
one. Through the very fact of this collaboration, the picture is an essential
element in the evolution of Florentine painting in the advance from the
fifteenth to the sixteenth century.

LEONARDO DA VINCI (1452–1519)   *Florentine School*
THE ANNUNCIATION   Panel
Inv. No. 1618   Height 98.5 cm. (38³/₄″)
                          Width 217.5 cm. (85⁵/₈″)

Until 1869 the picture was ascribed to Domenico Ghirlandaio. The attribution to Leonardo was validated chiefly through the discovery of a drawing, certainly by him, for a detail of the angel figure. Nevertheless, there are still some who will only allow that Leonardo helped in the execution of the painting, which undoubtedly came from Verrocchio's studio. As for its chronological placing, the *Annunciation* could predate the angel in Verrocchio's *Baptism*, though not by much. It is definitely an early work but one already packed with indications of what the painter's artistic personality would be when fully developed. These appear despite the persistence of Verrocchiesque forms in the Virgin and the marble table, whose similarity in decoration to the tomb of Piero and Giovanni de' Medici at San Lorenzo has rightly been pointed out. Where Leonardo's personality already bursts forth is in the drapery, which was always an object of special study for him, as is evident from the countless drawings of it that survive. In their exquisite sensitivity, the hands are related to those of Verrocchio's marble bust of a lady at the Bargello. The angel figure shows the originality and power of Leonardo's art even more clearly, in the delicate variation of the colours, in the gentleness of the attitude, in the beauty of the face, in the feathery posing on a flower-strewn lawn depicted with all his special love and care, and finally in the distant landscape, so romantic in the changeful light. The Louvre *Annunciation*, which is also undoubtedly Leonardesque, modifies the arrangement, particularly in the figure of the archangel. But through the very fact of having the dimensions of a predella panel, it does not, in spite of being our first evidence of the stylistic independence achieved by the painter, possess the intensity of suggestion found in the Uffizi picture, which alters the traditional layout of the scene.

    The work came from the monastery of Monteoliveto near Florence in 1867.

LEONARDO DA VINCI (1452–1519)   *Florentine School*
THE ADORATION OF THE MAGI   Panel
Inv. No. 1594   Height 243 cm. (95⁵/₈″)
                                 Width 246 cm. (96⁷/₈″)

The monks of San Donato a Scopeto commissioned Leonardo da Vinci in March 1481 to paint this picture for the high altar of their church. It was never finished by the artist, and according to Vasari it found its way to start with into 'the house of Amerigo Benci opposite the Loggia dei Peruzzi': Leonardo did a very lovely portrait of Amerigo's daughter, now in the collection of the Prince of Liechtenstein. In 1621 the *Adoration* was at the Medici Casino in the Via Larga, among the belongings of an illegitimate son of Grand Duke Francesco, Don Antonio de' Medici, of whose estate an inventory was being made. The collection of his son Don Giulio went, when he died, in 1670, to the Medici repository and from there to the Uffizi which it left only temporarily to be sent to the Villa of Castello before 1794.

The panel is no less perfect for being unfinished; for its fascination lies not only in the grandeur of the composition but also in the newness and unreality of the types, which bear that mark of superior humanity which would thereafter be common to all the figures Leonardo created. His vision is here realized through a range of tone values that build the entire scene in all its dimensions and gives it its spiritual meaning both as a whole and in every part. This spiritual meaning totally excludes all reference to previous iconographic tradition, whether in the movement that animates the whole crowd, in the originality of the architectural and landscape background, or in the light that picks out and defines the central group of the Virgin and Child.

As Leonardo had not finished the picture ordered from him, the monks commissioned Filippino Lippi to paint another, which was completed in 1495. Its subject is the same as the one given to Leonardo, and the measurements correspond almost exactly. This panel, which likewise is now at the Uffizi, shows that the artist must have kept in mind the unfinished work. Though good, it is naturally far from having the lofty poetry of Leonardo's *Adoration*, precisely because it is more human.

FRA BARTOLOMMEO DELLA PORTA (1474–1517) *Florentine School*
The Deposition   Panel
Inv. Palatina No. 64   Height 158 cm. (62¼")
                                               Width 199 cm. (78³/₈")

Vasari refers to this picture, saying that it was begun in the Augustinian church of San Gallo (no longer existent, as it was reduced to ruins during the siege of 1530) and that Giuliano Bugiardini finished it. He saw it on the high altar of San Jacopo tra' Fossi, at the Alberti corner. He mentions it again in his life of Bugiardini, asserting that the monk had 'left it only drawn in and shaded with watercolour on the gesso of the panel', and that Bugiardini had then painted it, including figures of St Peter and St Paul no longer visible. In actual fact, to judge by the quality, it seems obvious that the picture is in all essentials by Fra Bartolommeo and even one of his best; also, that the two figures now missing were an addition of Bugiardini's, which would explain their removal in the seventeenth of eighteenth century. Fiocco has reasonably suggested that one should see in the painting a reflection of Perugino's *Deposition* (also at the Pitti), which was unveiled in 1495. All the same, the derivations or the actual repetitions of details that can be observed in Fra Bartolommeo's picture do not detract from its originality, thanks to the new rhythm bestowed on the composition, the strong plasticity of Christ's body, and the fresh significance given to the scene by introducing St John the Evangelist.

This *Deposition* had in its turn an influence on contemporary artists, as is apparent from Andrea del Sarto's 1523 rendering of the subject, now likewise at the Pitti; yet it still remains unsurpassed for the novelty of the diagonal arrangement and the beauty and grandeur of the forms.

The picture belongs to Fra Bartolommeo's late period, after his return from Rome, round about 1515, and it indicates with the other works of the same years a return to the restraint and effectiveness of expression that had always been his best traits.

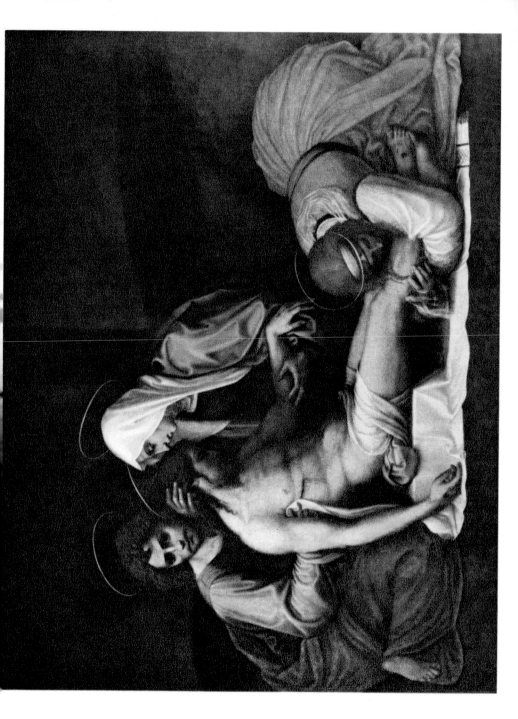

MARIOTTO ALBERTINELLI (1474–1515)
THE VISITATION
Inv. No. 1587

PREDELLA
Inv. No. 1586

Florentine School
Panel
Height 232.5 cm. (91¹/₂")
Width 146 cm. (57¹/₂")
Height 23 cm. (9")
Width 150 cm. (59")

The work is dated 1503. It was once in the Oratory of the Congregazione dei Preti della Visitazione at the church, since destroyed, of San Michele delle Trombe. Albertinelli was trained in Cosimo Rosselli's workshop, where he came to know Baccio della Porta, later Fra Bartolommeo, whose friendly advice determined many aspects of his art. In this picture, which is his masterpiece, he nonetheless established a personal style, different in form and colour, even if equally dependent on the teachings of Leonardo, who provided the model for all Florentine painters.

The isolation of the two figures against a background of open sky, which appears beyond the richly decorated arcading, gives the scene a new grandeur and a sense of calm inward poetry. Moreover, the strong hues and bright light display to the full the originality of Albertinelli's idea of colour as compared with the hitherto prevailing Florentine tradition.

The predella shows the *Annunciation,* the *Nativity,* and the *Presentation in the Temple.* It has more links with the fifteenth-century tradition, in the essential grace of the details, in the cheerful colours, and in the delicate profiles.

PIERO DI COSIMO (1462–1521)   *Florentine School*
PERSEUS FREEING ANDROMEDA   Panel
Inv. No. 1536   Height   71 cm.   (28")
                                                 Width   123 cm.   (48³/₈")

According to Vasari the picture was painted for Filippo Strozzi the elder and given by Giovan Battista di Lorenzo Strozzi to Sforza Almeni, a member of Duke Cosimo I's court. In 1589 it was already at the Uffizi, in the Tribuna, as is apparent from the inventory, which even says without foundation that it owes its design to Leonardo. On the other hand, it is a fact that Piero too was affected by Leonardo's technique and that here the figure grouping in particular is Leonardesque. But his other known works with mythological subjects confirm the attribution, owing to the originality of the composition, the understanding of nature shown in the landscape executed with exceptional care and delicacy, and the richness of the colour, which together make him one of the most individual artists of the Florentine School. Even from his earliest activity, various profane works are known in which lively fantasy alternates with movingly intimate passages and imaginary landscapes abounding in hints of poetry. This example at the Uffizi belongs to a later period, when the artist had already come under the influence of Northern prints, then circulating particularly widely in Italy, as can be seen above all from the landscape. Specially notable is the method of narration, which illustrates the successive incidents in the legend, thereby giving occasion for a balance of masses that makes still more evident the breadth and luminosity of the landscape, with its gradations of tone and its already Leonardesque *sfumato*.

At Florence there are three other scenes from the Perseus legend (now in the Davanzati Palace), which were once thought to be those painted, according to Vasari, for Francesco del Pugliese; but they do not have the vivacity and exquisite charm of this one.

RAPHAEL (RAPHAELLO SANZIO) (1483–1520)   *Italian School*
PORTRAIT OF AGNOLO DONI   Panel
Inv. Palatina No. 61   Height 63 cm. (24³/₄")
                                         Width 45 cm. (17³/₄")

This portrait was commissioned by Agnolo Doni, together with the one of his wife, during Raphael's second visit to Florence. Vasari saw them at the house of Agnolo's son Giovanbattista, and they remained in the Doni home till the eighteenth century. The last descendants of the family sold them to Grand Duke Leopold II of Tuscany in 1826 for 2,500 secchini.

Agnolo Doni married Maddalena Strozzi in 1503, and the portraits were presumably done during 1505–06, before Raphael left for Rome. In Agnolo's portrait the effects of the artist's stay in Florence are already evident; but the arrangement is still of a fifteenth-century type, and memories of fifteenth-century painting appear both in the individual character, which the artist makes every effort to render, and in the sobriety of the form, which it has been suggested recalls Domenico Ghirlandaio's portraits.

On the back of the panel there is a scene from the myth of Deucalion and Pyrrha, painted in monochrome: the gods on high and flooded Greece below, with her inhabitants struggling in the water. It was probably done by some assistant of Raphael's.

RAPHAEL (RAFFAELLO SANZIO) (1483–1520)   *Italian School*
THE MADONNA OF THE GOLDFINCH   Panel
Inv. No. 1447   Height 107 cm. (42¹/₈")
                                              Width   77 cm. (30¹/₄")

According to Vasari this Madonna was painted by Raphael for the marriage of a Florentine nobleman called Lorenzo Nasi, who was an intimate
friend of his; but on the ruin of the Nasi family in 1547 the picture
suffered very serious damage, the traces of which are still visible.

First recorded at the Uffizi in the inventory of 1704, this also is a work
from Raphael's Florentine period, datable to 1506. It can be said that
here even more than in other contemporary works Raphael has at last fully
assimilated the teachings of Florence, yet without in any way ceasing to
express truthfully his own personality. The pyramidal composition, which
derives from Fra Bartolommeo's examples, if not from Leonardo's too,
is among the most fully developed of its kind, and it makes use of a
landscape in which the figures are directly included, so that the former
contributed equally to that expressive compendium of a higher life which
contains the principal message of Raphael's creations. This motif was
to keep reappearing for a long time in his *œuvre*. Despite the basically
different pose and expression, the Uffizi picture is close in composition as
well as date to the so-called *Belle Jardinière* at the Louvre, another
example of the way Raphael liked to make the divine beings human in
spirit.

RAPHAEL (RAFFAELLO SANZIO) (1483–1520)   *Italian School*
THE LADY WITH A VEIL (LA DONNA VELATA)   Canvas
Inv. Palatina No. 245   Height 85 cm. (33¹/₂″)
                                           Width 64 cm. (25¹/₄″)

This very beautiful portrait is that of a woman loved by Raphael, so Vasari tell us, and in his day it was at the home of the Florentine merchant Matteo Botti. A descendant of Botti's, also called Matteo, left it when he died to Grand Duke Cosimo II de' Medici. From then on it formed part of the Medici collection, first in the Palazzo Pitti and then in the Villa del Poggio Imperiale, from which it returned to the Pitti in 1844.

The woman Vasari mentions is the famous Fornarina, so this is evidently a portrait of her, and there can now be no doubt about the identification or about the attribution to Raphael. It thus belongs to his Roman period and more exactly to that time around 1515, when the appeal of Venetian colour was at its strongest for him, and when other portraits appeared that also count among his greatest masterpieces.

The change in spirit the artist underwent on entering the Roman milieu is perceptible in the majesty emanating from the gesture and the lovely, exuberant forms, and in the ostentatious clothing, whose richness gives Raphael a chance to reveal himself as a colourist with a new vivacity and warmth. The symphony of grey and gold offered by this magnificent costume tremendously enhances the figure, which has an ideal, truly classical beauty.

Raphael painted another portrait of the Fornarina, which was once in the Barberini collection and now belongs to the Galleria Nazionale d'Arte Antica at Rome, though it is still at the Palazzo Barberini.

RAPHAEL (RAFFAELLO SANZIO) (1483–1520)   *Italian School*
THE MADONNA OF THE GRAND DUKE   Panel
Inv. Palatina No. 178   Height 84 cm. (33¹/₈″)
                                             Width 55 cm. (21⁵/₈″)

Grand Duke Ferdinando III of Tuscany bought this picture for 300 secchini on the art market in 1799, but its earlier provenance is not known. It was in the Pitti by 1828. Of the numerous Madonnas by Raphael it has the simplest layout, although this does not make it any less harmonious, in the calm expressed by the way the group is posed no less than by the two faces. The Virgin has the appropriate sweetness but also a thoughtful look that brings the figure even closer to what was most enduring in the tradition of fifteenth-century Florentine art, and not just painting.

We also see here the light, clear hues characteristic of the Florentine School—hues that accord admirably with the rhythm of the composition and contribute effectively to our impression of a truly divine image.

It is interesting that the Uffizi has a drawing for this Madonna in which she is placed in a circle. This may have been a first idea subsequently abandoned.

RAPHAEL (RAFFAELLO SANZIO) (1483–1520)   *Italian School*
THE MADONNA OF THE CHAIR   Panel
Inv. Palatino No. 151   Diam. 71 cm. (28″)

This painting was on show in 1589 in the Tribuna of the Uffizi, where it remained till the eighteenth century. It belongs to Raphael's Roman period and dates from 1516, being contemporary with the frescoes for the Stanza di Eliodoro at the Vatican and in particular with the one showing the *Mass of Bolsena,* in which the light, gay hues of the group of women and children beside the altar recall the charming colour of this Madonna.

The type of the Madonna is quite different from Raphael's early ones, which are mystical images of a divinity, whereas here we have a vigorous, sturdy mother, classically and sublimely beautiful. In all this is to be seen the influence of that antiquity which the artist admired so deeply in Rome, and which is so strongly reflected above all in the harmony, restraint, and clarity of his compositions. The group obtains complete unity from the balanced way the figures are inscribed in the circle according to a rhythm of curves that suits the picture's round form, which may be a memory of the Florentine period.

Here again the colour shows traces of Venetian influence, transmitted particularly through Sebastiano del Piombo, in its richness and airy freshness, and in a luminosity that Raphael now imparts with wonderful animation.

RAPHAEL (RAFFAELLO SANZIO) (1483–1520)   *Italian School*
PORTRAIT OF POPE LEO X WITH CARDINALS
GIULIO DE' MEDICI AND LUIGI DE' ROSSI   Panel
Inv. Palatina No. 40   Height 154 cm. (60⁵/₈")
                                               Width 119 cm. (46⁷/₈")

This portrait, which Vasari says was painted in Rome, must date back
to the years 1517/19, because de' Rossi was made a cardinal in 1517 and
died in 1519. Having probably passed to the Medici family after the Pope's
death (Federico II Gonzaga saw it over a door at the Casa Medici), it
was given by Alessandro to Ottaviano de' Medici and then by him to
Duke Cosimo I, so that it was in the grand-ducal repository in Vasari's
day and in the Tribuna of the Uffizi in 1589.

It is the outstanding work of Raphael's late period, an 'impressive
architecture of setting and figures' that overwhelms us with the powerful
unity of its plastic form, which still expresses all the grandeur characteristic of his greatest works.

Both the cardinals standing beside the Pope were related to him. Giulio
de' Medici was the son of Lorenzo the Magnificent's brother Giuliano,
killed in 1478 during the Pazzi Conspiracy, and he was to mount the
throne of St Peter in 1523 as Clement VII. For him Raphael saw to the
building of the Villa Madama and painted his last work, the *Transfiguration*, still unfinished when he died. The other, Luigi de' Rossi, was the son
of an illegitimate son of Piero the Gouty, and he became a cardinal thanks
to being a kinsman of the Pope, with whom he had been educated. Yet
he did not have a big hand in papal policy owing to his untimely death,
which greatly saddened Leo X.

In its association of the two cardinals with the figure of the Pope, this
portrait is already grandiosely sixteenth century, but above all it
marks the climax of Raphael's portraiture, through the completely
original interpretation of those represented and the total independence of
all precedents—even the artist's own—which are transcended in the
search for a perfection that goes beyond any stylistic or formal achievements. This is a true glorification by Raphael of the Pope who had been
such an affectionate and satisfactory patron to him.

A contemporary copy of the portrait exists, done by Andrea del Sarto
for Federico II, Duke of Mantua.

LORENZO DI CREDI (1459–1537)   *Florentine School*
THE ANNUNCIATION AND THREE SCENES FROM GENESIS
Inv. No. 1597   Panel
                                                      Height 88 cm. (34⁵/₈")
                                                      Width 71.5 cm. (28¹/₈")

This picture dates from the years immediately after 1480. In spite of being very early, it is among the artist's most beautiful works, through its force of expression and refinement of execution. Lorenzo's training beside Leonardo and Perugino in Andrea del Verrocchio's workshop accounts for the Leonardo influence already apparent in this *Annunciation*, above all in the figure of the angel. What predominates in his works is a calm and undramatic interpretation of the religious theme, which is expressed through an attempt to rise towards his ideal of beauty and through a bent for compositions with a closed rhythm, where even the landscape plays an essential part in the representation. This picture's delicacy of both form and colour was perhaps never achieved again in any of his other certain works that remain to us.

Below, the three scenes in chiaroscuro of the *Creation of Eve,* the *Fall of Man,* and the *Expulsion from Paradise,* serve to heighten the significance of the main scene with its presage of the Redemption. The altarpiece comes from the collection left in 1675 by Cardinal Leopoldo de' Medici. From the grand-ducal repository it entered the Uffizi in 1798.

ANDREA DEL SARTO (1486–1530)
THE DISPUTE ON THE HOLY TRINITY
Inv. Palatina No. 172

Florentine School
Panel
Height 232 cm. (91³/₈")
Width 193 cm. (76")

When Andrea del Sarto received the commission to paint this picture, he had already, according to Vasari, done two others for the friars of San Gallo fuor della Porta Ominima: a *Christ with St Mary Magdalen* and an *Annunciation*, which is also at the Pitti. The four standing figures represent SS. Augustine, Lawrence, Peter Martyr, and Francis; below, kneeling, are St Sebastian and Mary Magdalen.

After the destruction of the church during the siege of 1530 the painting was taken to San Jacopo tra' Fossi, but it was in the Palazzo Pitti by 1681, when Baldinucci wrote his *Notizie dei professori del disegno.* The work is considered to date from just after 1517, when the artist had completed the first part of the fresco cycle for the Chiostro dello Scalzo and painted the *Madonna of the Harpies,* now at the Uffizi.

It is a very noble composition in the expressive intensity of the faces, the stately poses, the excellent proportions of the forms, and the impressive drapery. The harmonious arrangement of the figures shows a perfect balance and effectively conveys even the spiritual meaning of the conversation taking place. Delicate, muted colours and transparent glazes give the modelling a softness that makes this one of the most perfect works Andrea has left us; yet the loving care of the execution does not reduce in the slightest the profundity of the idea behind the subject, which is why we can echo the praise bestowed on the pictures by Vasari and all later critics.

MICHELANGELO BUONARROTI (1475–1564)   *Florentine School*
THE HOLY FAMILY   Panel
Inv. No. 1456   Diam. 120 cm. (47¹/₄")

This tondo was painted in 1504 for the wedding of Agnolo Doni and Maddalena Strozzi, whose portraits by Raphael are to be seen at the Palazzo Pitti. The three crescents from the armorial bearings of the Strozzi family of Florence are worked into the carving on the very beautiful original frame. From the hand-written inventory of 1635, it appears that the tondo was in the Tribuna of the Uffizi by that date. This is the earliest known painting by Michelangelo, who here already reveals his whole personality and his particular vision of plastic form. Moreover, it is the only one, apart from the frescoes, that is certainly authentic, as the *Manchester Madonna* at the National Gallery, London, is now considered a studio work and the unfinished *Entombment*, also at the National Gallery, is also excluded by almost every critic from the list of Michelangelo's works.

It has been observed that the motif of the nudes in the background could have been inspired by Signorelli's *Virgin and Child* at the Uffizi, and that the landscape may derive from certain Flemish models. Nevertheless, Michelangelo's picture-structure disregards all iconographic links and achieves the firmness of architecture in the characteristic spiral movement of the central group, which is wonderfully modelled with a sculptural clarity. The figures have been conceived as forms that may be termed 'supernatural', such is the power that animates them and the truly divine calm expressed by their faces; and this marvellously unified group stands out against a landscape background constructed with a few essential lines and peopled by nudes that have rightly been seen as a reflection of the lost cartoon for the *Battle of Cascina*, with which Michelangelo was then occupied, and as a prefiguration of the Sistine nudes. The colour accompanies and interprets the forms, accentuating their contrasted masses, while the chiaroscuro heightens their relief. Everything thus combines to increase the imposing monumentality of this composition.

164

ROSSO FIORENTINO (Giovanni Battista di Jacopo) (1494–1541)

Florentine School

MOSES DEFENDING THE DAUGHTERS OF JETHRO

Canvas

Inv. No. 2151

Height 160 cm. (63")
Width 117 cm. (46¹/₈")

Vasari says that Rosso painted this picture for Giovanni Bandini (not to be confused with the Florentine sculptor of the same name) and praises its very fine nudes. The scene is of Moses striking the shepherds who have driven from the well the daughters of his father-in-law Jethro, priest of Midian.

Rosso's Michelangelesque tendency does not attenuate the freshness of his imagination. He shows both assurance in the design and inventiveness in his sense of colour, which favours iridescences and arresting light effects. In this work, painted after his stay at Rome, there are also reflections of the Roman milieu and of antique sculpture, which make it less forced and introduce classical poses. The picture must date from round about 1525 and is notable above all for the originality of the colour scheme, based entirely on contrasts between hues and on variety in the planes of light. It surpasses all his earlier experiments, from the Volterra *Depostion* to the *Virgin and Child* for Santo Spirito and the *Marriage of the Virgin* for San Lorenzo. The vividness and brilliance of the hues does not conceal the subtlety of their relationships, and the colour enhances the movement of the figures.

The other Bible scene showing Rebecca and Eliezer at the well, that Vasari mentions together with this one may be a work now in the Museo Nazionale di San Matteo at Pisa, though some believe the latter is just a copy.

As Rosso went to France, where he became the King's official painter, his reputation in Italy did not immediately equal his merit; only in recent times has it been permanently established by the critics.

The work comes from the collection left by Don Antonio de' Medici in 1632.

BACHIACCA (Francesco di Ubertino) (1494–1557)   *Florentine School*
ST MARY MAGDALEN   Panel
Inv. Palatina No. 102   Height 51 cm. (20¹/₈")
                                                Width 42 cm. (16¹/₂")

Bachiacca, a pupil of Perugino and Franciabigio, came under the influence
of Andrea del Sarto and Michelangelo. Highly praised by Vasari,
'especially in doing small figures, which he executed perfectly', he
collaborated with Pontormo, Andrea del Sarto, and Granacci on the
cassoni and *spalliere* for Pier Francesco Borgherini's room and with
Franciabigio on works for Giovan Maria Benintendi's.

The *St Mary Magdalen* was already in the grand-ducal collections
during Cosimo III's reign, between 1713 and 1723. At that time it was
assigned to the school of Leonardo da Vinci, which explains the subsequent attribution to Aurelio Luini, son of the more famous Bernardino.
Bernard Berenson claimed it for Bachiacca, and it does in fact have the
rosy flesh tints with cool shadows characteristic of his figures. The
female type also often crops up in other works by him, such as the
Berlin *Beheading of St John the Baptist* or the *Moses* formerly in the
Bardini collection.

This *St Mary Magdalen* constitutes one of the most successful moments
in Bachiacca's art, which is full of preciosities and aims at a dainty
refinement of form and colour. Following a custom already established
in Florence, this is a portrait given the attributes of a saint. It should be
compared with the one at the Museo di Palazzo Venezia, Rome, which
may also be intended to represent the Magdalen and is no less refined
and elegant.

PONTORMO (Jacopo Carrucci) (1494–1557)   *Florentine School*
PORTRAIT OF COSIMO DE' MEDICI, *Pater Patriae*   Panel
Inv. No. 3574   Height 87 cm. (34¹/₄″)
Width 65 cm. (25⁵/₈″)

Painted for Goro Cheri da Pistoia, secretary to Lorenzo de' Medici, Duke of Urbino, the portrait belonged in Vasari's day to Alessandro di Ottaviano de' Medici (later Pope Leo XI), after which it spent some time in the cell known as Cosimo's at the friary of San Marco, Florence. It was presumably painted during 1518 and 1519, the latter being the year of Lorenzo's death.

As for the iconography, it may go back to those anonymous Florentine medals (cf. page 113: Botticelli's *Portrait of a Man with a Medal*) showing Cosimo the Elder with the title *Pater Patriae;* but in the Old Sacristy of San Lorenzo there is a coloured terracotta relief that Pontormo may also have followed. Since it is a posthumous portrait, one rightly notices a certain idealization of the sitter, who was well suited to it by the glory that surrounded him and that remained extremely bright in Florence despite the political vicissitudes, and by the undying memory of him as the founder of both Florentine and Medicean power. This very fine but austere image can thus be said to constitute, partly by reason of the vibrantly energetic forms, a true glorification of the man who had earned the right to be called father of his country. It also provides an example of Pontormo's tendency to use colour for enhancing line, sometimes to the point of making it a principal element, with the verve and elasticity of the lines matched by the brightness and strength of the hues.

It was in consequence of the order for this portrait that Ottaviano de' Medici, who managed the property of his distant cousins in their absence, commissioned Pontormo to adorn the reception room of the villa at Poggio a Caiano. There the artist left what is perhaps his most notable work, thanks to the fresh interpretation of reality and the perfect decorative unity.

AGNOLO BRONZINO (1502–1572) *Florentine School*
PORTRAIT OF ELEONORA OF TOLEDO WITH HER SON GIOVANNI Panel
Inv. No. 748 Height 115 cm. (45¹/₄")
Width 96 cm. (37³/₄")

Eleonora of Toledo married Duke Cosimo I in 1539 and died in 1562; her son Giovanni was born in 1543 and also died in 1562. The portrait is mentioned in the 1553 inventory of Duke Cosimo's repository, but the boy is identified there as Francesco. However, a comparison with other images of Cosimo's sons leads one to believe that he is actually Giovanni, which accords with Vasari's reference in the second edition of his *Lives*. Hence the picture must date from between 1543 and 1553—from the period, that is, when Bronzino was working on Eleonora's chapel in the Palazzo Vecchio. It is certainly one of his loveliest portraits and among those most representative of his art.

Though Eleonora's bearing is stiffly majestic, she has a rather sad expression, and Bronzino has here created an image absolutely perfect in its form and coloured with deep sensitivity. The luxuriousness of the costume, the severity of the background, and the stateliness of the figure do not conflict with each other, but interpenetrate as one single fresh vision, in which the form has an exquisitely decorative role. There is a piece of material in the Franchetti collection at the Bargello that is almost exactly like the magnificent fabric of Eleonora's dress.

The painting came to the Uffizi from the Medici Villa of la Petraia in 1798.

GIORGIO VASARI (1511–1574)   *Florentine School*
PORTRAIT OF LORENZO THE MAGNIFICENT   Panel
Inv. No. 1578   Height 90 cm. (35³/₈″)
                                           Width 72.5 cm. (28¹/₂″)

Owned in Vasari's day by Ottaviano de' Medici, this portrait is listed
as being at the Uffizi in the hand-written inventory of 1784. Vasari says
in his memoirs that it was done in 1534 for Ottaviano, but it was actually
intended for Alessandro de' Medici, as is proved by a letter to the Duke
from Vasari himself, who there explains just how he is going to execute
it.

Probably to indulge the taste for pomp, and following the heroic style
of its time, the portrait is not quite as faithful as the earlier representations,
and all the study that went into the plan certainly has not helped to
make the composition look spontaneous. Nevertheless, the many allegorical
attributes surrounding the figure do not stand out too much from the
background, and so do not reduce the prominence of the figure, with its
rather hard lines and its pose that is less static than that of the preceding
likeness of Alessandro de' Medici. As a posthumous portrait, it undoubtedly lacks the force of the fifteenth-century images, like the one on
Niccolò Fiorentino's medal, but it still has an uncontrived expressiveness,
as can best be seen from a preparatory drawing in the Gabinetto dei
Disegni at the Uffizi.

175

GIORGIONE *(Giorgio Barbarelli da Castelfranco)* (1478–1511)
Venetian School
THE INFANT MOSES BEFORE PHARAOH FOR THE TRIAL OF GOLD AND FIRE
Panel
Inv. No. 945 Height 90 cm. (35⅝")
Width 71.8 cm. (28¼")

Along with the *Judgment of Solomon,* this picture is described in an inventory of the Villa del Poggio Imperiale dating from 1692, but without any attribution. It came from the villa to the Uffizi in 1795 as a Giovanni Bellini. The attribution to Giorgione, first made by Cavalcaselle, has been vigorously contested in both cases, one of its most recent challengers being Fiocco. While admitting the Giorgionesque character of the figures and landscape, and even of the legendary subject, he ends by saying that the Moses picture appears to have been designed by Giorgione, who probably executed the central group and a good deal of the landscape, but that the rest is due to Giulio Campagnola, a Paduan artist closely connected with the master. Venturi suggests an anonymous follower of Giorgione not yet able to free himself from fifteenth-century norms. Today it seems more reasonable to think that the *Trial* is wholly authentic and the *Judgment,* at least largely so. In any case, it is a question of early works, datable to the period 1498–1500, that merit admiration above all for the originality of their poetic conception as a lyrical rendering of dramatic events. This is achieved both through the landscape and through the figures inserted in it to form a unified composition that has a truly romantic beauty.

One is also led to such a view by a comparison with Giorgione's certain works, like the *Tempest,* the Castelfranco *Madonna,* or the *Judith,* where one meets again facial forms and effects of space in the landscape whose starting-point is already there in these small early pictures.

TITIAN *(Tiziano Vecellio)* (c. 1490–1576)   *Venetian School*
THE CONCERT   Canvas
Inv. Palatina No. 185   Height 109 cm. (42⁷/₈″)
                                                Width 123 cm. (48³/₈″)

This picture was acquired in 1654 by Cardinal Leopoldo de' Medici from
Paolo del Sera, a Florentine nobleman living at Venice, as the work of
Giorgione da Castelfranco. At one time it was suspected that it might
be identical with a picture representing the same subject and by the
same artist that was in the Tribuna in 1597, during the reign of
Grand Duke Ferdinando I de' Medici; but the description of Ridolfi,
who mentions it as the property of Del Sera in 1648, rules out this
hypothesis. The attribution to Giorgione, corroborated by other seventeenth-century sources, was not questioned until the last decades of the
nineteenth century, when Giovanni Morelli thought he could see in it an
early work by Titian. After that, critical opinion was divided: some
writers put forward other names, such as Sebastiano del Piombo or
Domenico Campagnola, but most approved Morelli's suggestion, which
today finds almost universal acceptance. In point of fact the dramatic
energy radiating from the face of the harpsichord-player is very Titian-
like, as are the firm construction of the figures and the unity of the
composition concentrated in the group dominated by the central figure of
the performer. Some have tried to see in this picture a collaboration
between Titian and Giorgione, which would mean that Giorgione was the
senior partner. But it is more likely that the work took its rise in the
imagination of Titian alone, at a time when he had not yet completely
freed himself from Giorgione's influence, as would occur with the Frari
Assumption.

TITIAN (Tiziano Vecellio) (c. 1490–1576)   *Venetian School*
PORTRAIT OF A MAN   Canvas
Inv. Palatina No. 92   Height 143 cm. (56¼")
                                                  Width 93 cm. (36⅝")

This picture also came from Urbino, even though it cannot be recognized
in any of those described in the inventory of the works sent from Urbino
to Florence; it could, on the other hand, be one in a list of the best
paintings inherited by Vittoria della Rovere.

Once again the identity of the subject is uncertain. At one time he was
thought, quite without foundation, to be a member of the Howard
family (Dukes of Norfolk), and for a while the portrait went by the name
of the *Young Englishman.* Then someone suggested that it represented
Guidobaldo II, Duke of Urbino, of whom Titian is known to have done
two portraits; but a comparison with others of the Duke shows this
theory to be unsound as well. Adolfo Venturi thought he could recognize
in it the jurisconsult Ippolito Riminaldi, on the grounds of another portrait
now at the Accademia di San Luca in Rome. Yet this identification is
unacceptable, too, as the differences, above all psychological, between the
two figures exceed the superficial resemblances. More recently it has been
claimed that the picture shows Ottavio Farnese, of whose family Titian
was the favourite portraitist. In that case it would have to be placed
between 1547 and 1552, instead of between 1540 and 1545 as was previously thought.

At all events, it is one of the finest portraits Titian has left us, for the
life that emanates miraculously from the severe face; for the perfect forms,
the vigorous colour, and the intriguing light; but especially for the power
the artist has attained, leaving aside all ordinary expressive means and
creating a living image that transcends reality.

TITIAN (Tiziano Vecellio) (c. 1490–1576)   *Venetian School*
FLORA   Canvas
Inv. No. 1462   Height 79 cm. (31¹/₈″)
Width 63 cm. (24³/₄″)

We do not know for whom this wonderful image was painted. During the first half of the seventeenth century it belonged to a Spanish ambassador in Amsterdam, Don Alfonso Lopez, who sold it to Archduke Leopoldo Wilhelm of Austria, Governor of the Netherlands (died 1662). After being in the Archduke's collection, it went to Vienna and came from the Imperial Gallery there to the Uffizi in 1793, when an exchange of pictures occurred.

The name 'Flora' as a title for the work goes back to a seventeenth-century engraving by Joachim Sandrart. This allegorical interpretation is not entirely groundless, for we see a figure whose beauty is more generalized than individual. It cannot, therefore, just be the portrait of a bride, as Burckhardt thought on comparing it with images in contemporary Venetian books on costume. Here we have, rather, an ideal costume, and it belongs to the loveliest of the gentle figures of Venetian women that Titian depicted during his early period, such as the *Salome* in the Galleria Doria, the Louvre *Lady at the Mirror*, or the Munich *Vanity*.

The *Flora* is undoubtedly closer to the Frari *Assumption* than to the Treviso *Annunciation* and can thus be placed round about 1520 at the latest, if, indeed, it should not be brought back to 1515.

This ideal of womanly beauty was to remain characteristic of Titian, spreading from him to much of the Venetian painting of his day. But no one else would achieve the perfection of the face, the flawless proportions of the sturdy body, the grace of the pose, and the chromatic richness of the hair, which together put this among the masterpieces of all painting, irrespective of place or time.

TITIAN (Tiziano Vecellio) (c. 1490–1576) St Mary Magdalen Inv. Palatina No. 67

Venetian School Panel Height 84 cm. (33¹/₈″) Width 69 cm. (27¹/₈″)

This is another picture that came to the Medici family with the Della Rovere inheritance. It must be the one seen by Vasari in the repository of Francesco Maria I, Duke of Urbino: 'a half-length figure of St Mary Magdalen with her hair loose, which is a remarkable work'.

Although there is no trace of this panel in the Urbino documents, Carlo Ridolfi mentions in his *Meraviglie dell'arte*, which is among the most important sources for Venetian art, a *Magdalen* that Titian was said to have painted at Urbino for the Duke. Since we know from a letter of 1531 from Federico II Gonzaga that Titian painted at his request, a *Penitent Magdalen*, which was sent to Vittoria Colonna's husband the Marquis del Vasto, some have suspected that the Pitti work might be a second version of it. The picture bears the artist's signature on the ointment jar beside the saint. It has also been thought that the figure might go back to an antique Venus, which would not be out of keeping with Titian, who shows a knowledge of ancient sculpture in other works as well, or with this Magdalen, who is in fact a very beautiful sinner, but not too deeply religious.

There is a seventeenth-century copy in the Galleria Doria at Rome, ascribed to Sassoferrato. The *Magdalen* in the Hermitage at Leningrad, of which many replicas exist, may be regarded as a redevelopment of the Florentine one towards more concentrated expressiveness and increased grandeur. Though the pose is still the same, there is no longer that brightness in the complexion, that golden gleam in the hair, and that radiance in the sky, which are the chief merits of the Florence *Magdalen*.

TITIAN (Tiziano Vecellio) (c. 1490–1576)   *Venetian School*
La Bella (Portrait of a Woman)   Canvas
Inv. Palatina No. 18   Height 89 cm. (35")
                                                     Width 75 cm. (29½")

This picture too came with the inheritance from Urbino in 1632, and in all likelihood it is identical with the portrait of 'that lady with the blue dress' mentioned by Duke Francesco Maria I della Rovere in a letter of May 1536. The possibility that it is a youthful likeness of the Duke's wife Eleonora Gonzaga is now excluded, partly because the same woman appears in the *Venus of Urbino,* as is confirmed by the inventory of the pictures sent to Florence. Just as unconvincing is the theory that it may be the portrait of Isabella d'Este whom Titian painted between 1534 and 1536, even if the picture probably does date from about that time. So we must resign ourselves to not knowing who is represented in this work, typical of the best period of Titian's portraits, in which the colour creates the individual atmosphere that becomes the essential ingredient.

Here the principal hue is the dark greenish blue lit by gold of the brocaded dress; it is wonderfully harmonized with the violet of the sleeves and the white of the puffs scattered over them, and attuned to the complexion and blond hair of this very lovely woman. The figure owes its charm not only to the perfection of its features but even more to the vital accord expressed by the whole image, which is no longer impersonal and beyond time but an interpretation of something earthly and real.

For this portrait Titian also had to prepare a timpano, one of those canvases painted with some allegory that served to cover the most valuable works: Duke Francesco Maria mentions it in the letter in which he presses the artist for the picture. Of these covers, which are unlikely to have survived until our times, only three examples are known, including a Titianesque one for the portrait of Sperone Speroni.

TITIAN (Tiziano Vecellio) (c. 1490–1576)   *Venetian School*
THE VENUS OF URBINO   Canvas
Inv. No. 1437   Height 119.5 cm. (47″)
                                                Width 165 cm. (65″)

The painting came to Florence in 1631 with the collection left by the last duke of Urbino to Vittoria della Rovere, the fiancée and then the wife of Grand Duke Ferdinando II de' Medici. If this is the picture mentioned by Vasari as being in the repository of Francesco Maria I della Rovere, it must have been done before 1538, the date of the Duke's death; if it is the one referred to in a letter of the same year, 1538, from his son Guidobaldo, who is sending a messenger to Venice with orders to bring back 'the nude woman' Titian owes him, then it will have been executed for Guidobaldo, which could lend plausibility to the theory (even though this is not supported by solid evidence) that it shows one of his mistresses. The same person appears in the portrait of the so-called *La Bella* at the Pitti, and in that of the young woman wearing a fur, at Vienna. Hence the Uffizi picture must have been finished round about 1538, like the two just mentioned.

No longer is the female type idealized as in the *Flora:* more sensual, this woman is conscious of her own beauty, and the painter has thoroughly enjoyed modelling the body that stands out with its well-rounded limbs against the colours of the curtain, the couch, and the sheet. Nevertheless, of all Titian's *Venuses* this—the earliest known to us—is closest to the one by Giorgione at Dresden, above all because of the motif, which obviously derives from it despite the realism of the setting, the intimate nature of the scene, and the greater individualization of the figure, which in the Giorgione, as in the *Flora,* is impersonal and timeless.

188

TITIAN *(Tiziano Vecellio)* (c. 1490–1576)   *Venetian School*
                                                        Canvas
PORTRAIT OF PIETRO ARETINO   Height 98 cm. (38⁵/₈")
Inv. Palatina No. 54   Width 78 cm. (30³/₄")

This picture was given by Pietro Aretino to Duke Cosimo I de' Medici
in 1545, the year when Titian painted it: we learn this from Vasari and
from Aretino himself in one of his letters. Vasari adds that it is finer than
the other portrait Titian did in 1541 for his friend Francesco Marcolini,
the famous printer; and Aretino, in a letter to Paolo Giovio, calls it an
'awe-inspiring marvel'. It is indeed the most powerful of the portraits
from this period. Titian has here instilled the subject's character into
the pictorial form, building the image on a contrast of red and green,
and achieving perfect unity through his spontaneous and spirited brush-
work. The impression of force created by the figure with irresistible
directness conveys most effectively the personality of the subject as it is
known from his writings and from tradition. We really have here an
unsurpassed example of the biographical type of portrait that became
increasingly prominent during the sixteenth century.

In the letter accompanying the gift to Duke Cosimo, and in another to
Titian, Aretino complains that the artist has reproduced the materials of
the costume badly and done a sketch rather than a finished picture. But
knowing from his written works Aretino's taste for and understanding of
Titian's art on all occasions, one must regard these remarks as just another
of the many eccentricities of this strange man.

Veneto School

THE SO-CALLED FORNARINA

Inv. No. 1443

Panel

Height 68 cm. (26³/₄")
Width 54.5 cm. (21¹/₂")

The picture was in the Tribuna of the Uffizi in 1589 as a Raphael. It was ascribed to Giorgione, however, in the inventories of the seventeenth and eighteenth centuries. During the nineteenth it was once more thought to be by Raphael, until Giovanni Morelli proved towards the end of the century that it was really the work of a Giorgione pupil, Sebastiano del Piombo. As it is dated 1512 it belongs to the artist's first period.

The nineteenth-century identification of the young woman as the Fornarina loved by Raphael was shown some time ago to be incorrect, partly because of her appearance of noble rank and her rich costume. Vasari says that in Luca Torrigiani's home at Florence there was a portrait by Sebastiano of a woman 'in Roman clothes', but it does not seem that this can be the one in the Medici collection by 1589.

When he painted the Uffizi portrait, the painter had already met Raphael at Rome, and here he reveals his influence, which explains the original attribution. Nevertheless, there are still traces of the Venetian training of the artist, who had first studied under Giovanni Bellini, then under Giorgione. From the latter he has taken above all the posture of the bust, while the colour and plasticity reflect his classicizing tendencies, present since his early works. We thus see a blending of the Giorgione tradition with the style of Raphael, but it does not submerge the essential freshness of Sebastiano's personality, here displayed at one of his most successful moments.

Apart from the picture by Raphael at the Galleria Nazionale (Palazzo Barberini) in Rome, the real Fornarina portrait is the one at the Pitti, also by Raphael, called *The Lady with a Veil* (see page 153).

LORENZO LOTTO (c. 1476–1555/6)   *Veneto School*
SACRED CONVERSATION (Sacra Conversazione)   Canvas
Inv. No. 893   Height 87 cm. (34¹/₄″)
Width 69.5 cm. (27³/₈″)

Signed and dated 1534, this picture shows the Virgin and Child with
SS. Anne, Joachim, and Jerome. The Virgin is in St Anne's lap and
holds the Child to her, while Joachim faces them on the left, looking
intently at his grandson, and St Jerome stands behind him. Berenson has
remarked on the uneven quality of this painting, which seems to have been
executed 'in a moment of peculiar tension and displays a great nervous-
ness of movement as well as an exaggerated expressiveness and eagerness
in the faces, while at the same time the drawing is very loose'. It should
be noted that Lotto has here returned to a compositional theme already
treated on other occasions, but as always he has completely renovated
the forms. This goes not only for the *Sacra Conversazione* as a whole,
a subject very dear to this artist and to Venetian painters of the period
generally, but also for the group of St Anne with the Virgin and Child,
which follows a tradition reaching back at least to the fourteenth century
in Italy. Here Lotto has given an original interpretation of it but kept
intact that religious sense which is the main feature of all his work.
His vision of colour is more delicate and vibrant in the prevailing luminosity of the atmosphere, but it still remains personal vis-a-vis Venetian
painting, even though this acted as a stimulus on him.

The picture belongs to Lotto's middle period, which may be described
as essentially Venetian. In the figure of Joachim we may perhaps behold
the artist, on account of its resemblance to the portrait Ridolfi gives of
him.

The work came to the Uffizi from the grand-ducal repository in 1798.

TINTORETTO (Jacopo Robusti) (1518–1594)   *Venetian School*
THE MADONNA OF THE CONCEPTION   Canvas
Inv. Palatina No. 313   Height 151 cm. (59½")
Width 98 cm. (38⅝")

This picture came with the legacy of Cardinal Leopoldo de' Medici (1675), who had acquired it at Venice in 1658 through Paolo del Sera as a work by Tintoretto. Baldinucci mentioned its presence in the grand-ducal gallery as early as 1681.

According to some writers it is probably a fragment of a larger composition similar to that at Berlin with the Virgin, the Child, and the Evangelists Mark and Luke, or to that in the Accademia, Venice, with the Virgin, the Child, and SS. Marina, Cecilia, Theodore, Cosmas, and Damian. The Pitti painting is nevertheless earlier than the Berlin (1570–80) as well as the Venice (1580–90) one and must be assigned rather to the decade 1560–70, when the artist had already begun working in the Scuola di San Rocco. It has been pointed out that the figure of the Virgin contains a memory of Michelangelo's *Virgin* for the Medici Chapel.

The oblique composition is characteristic of Tintoretto's imagination and does not conflict with the theory that the painting formed part of a *Sacra Conversazione* like the one at Venice, in which this theme, traditional to Venetian painting, has been boldly transformed.

196

TINTORETTO *(Jacopo Robusti)* (1518–1594) *Venetian School*
PORTRAIT OF JACOPO SANSOVINO (1486–1570) Canvas
Inv. No. 957 Height 70 cm. (27⁵/₈″)
Width 65.5 cm. (25³/₄″)

In his *Riposo* (1584) Borghini says that this portrait was owned by Grand Duke Francesco. Mentioned in the gallery inventory of 1635–38, it was then on show in the Tribuna of the Uffizi. The work entered the repository in 1677, returning to the gallery in 1798. It has been conjectured that this portrait was brought to Florence in 1566, when Sansovino, then eighty, was elected a member of the Accademia delle Arti del Disegno together with Palladio and Titian. Others have believed that the Grand Duke commissioned it to preserve the memory of this Tuscan artist who settled at Venice.

Tintoretto has here given us one of his most animated portraits, executed with a precision and care that in no way detract from the impromptu character of the creation, from the amazing expression and life in the sitter's eyes, mouth, and hand. On stylistic grounds the work can be dated between 1560 and 1570—to the period, that is, of the paintings for the Sala dell' Albergo in the Scuola di San Rocco. It is undoubtedly among the most interesting of the many portraits Tintoretto has left us, and the theory, already put forward elsewhere, that Vasari had it before him when he did an equally lively portrait of Sansovino for his *Lives* is not implausible. Nevertheless, one still feels that the artist has transfigured the sitter according to his own vision and sensibility.

The versions in the Weimar Museum and a private collection at Florence are both replicas of the Uffizi picture. There is another Tintoretto portrait of Sansovino in a Dutch private collection: it shows him much less advanced in years and is therefore presumably earlier, in spite of having been assigned to about 1570.

199

PAOLO VERONESE (Paolo Caliari) (1528-1588) · *Veneto School*
PORTRAIT OF A NOBLEMAN · Canvas
Inv. Palatina No. 216 · Height 140 cm. (58¹/₈")
Width 107 cm. (42¹/₈")

This magnificent portrait also comes from the estate of Cardinal Leopoldo de' Medici. It is mentioned in a letter of 1659 to the Cardinal from Paolo del Sera, who says that it has cost him 300 silver scudi, but that he does not know whether it has reached Cardinal Leopoldo or his brother Cardinal Giovan Carlo. The subject was once thought to be Danielo Barbaro (1513–70), the prelate and learned humanist for whom and for whose brother Palladio built the villa at Maser, which Veronese decorated with wonderful frescoes; but the discovery of a documented portrait of him in a Dutch collection has ruled out this identification.

All the same, the person represented must be someone very important in the Venetian Republic, on account of the dignity he shows and the magnificence of his costume; and the fact that Veronese was chosen to convey his appearance is proof of this man's interest and artistic taste. Veronese has here achieved a monumentality superior to that of many of his other portraits. It springs from the harmonious, impressive composition and from the spatial and perspective arrangement of the figures no less than from the unity of the colouring, with its general severity, and from the stateliness of the almost sculptural pose. The effect of the silvery fur flowing from the mantle shows tremendous decorative imagination and helps to emphasize the man's calm face.

This portrait must have been painted around 1560, just about the time of the frescoes for the villa at Maser and of the portrait of a young man with a greyhound at the Metropolitan Museum, New York.

PAOLO VERONESE *(Paolo Caliari)* (1528-1588)   *Veneto School*
THE HOLY FAMILY WITH ST BARBARA   Canvas
Inv. No. 1433   Height 86 cm. (33$^7/_8$")
                                            Width 122 cm. (48")

Ridolfi says in his *Meraviglie dell' arte* (1648) that he saw this painting
at the home of the Counts Widmann (rich aristocratic merchants from
Carinthia with a famous collection of pictures), from whom it was bought
by Paolo del Sera, who resold it in 1654 to Cardinal Leopoldo de'
Medici. The canvas entered the grand-ducal repository with the collection
left by the Cardinal in 1675 and came to the Uffizi in 1798. It dates
from the decade 1560–70, thus following the great altarpiece for the
church of San Zaccaria, highly original through its diagonal composition,
now at the Accademia, Venice.

The Uffizi picture, in which the figures of the Virgin and St Barbara
enclose the Child while the other two are in shadow, is also very remarkable. Its golden-toned colour harmony heightens the impressiveness of the
two female figures as they stand out resplendent against the background,
with their sparkling silk dresses and gold-gleaming hair. The contrast
between the figure of the Virgin, simpler despite the still richly coloured
attire, and that of St Barbara, more sumptuous and more bathed in light,
increases the relief of the composition and makes its depth more evident.

CORREGGIO *(Antonio Allegri)* (c. 1489–1534) *Emilian School*
THE VIRGIN ADORING THE CHILD   Canvas
Inv. No. 1453   Height 81 cm. (31⁷/₈")
                                        Width 67 cm. (26³/₈")

The picture entered the gallery on 6 November 1617 as a gift from
Ferdinando Gonzaga, Duke of Mantua, to Cosimo de' Medici. It dates
from the artist's maturity, after the frescoes for the Camera di San Paolo,
if not also after those in the dome of San Giovanni Evangelista at Parma.
Accordingly, it can be placed round about 1520–22 owing to similarities
with other pictures of this period and shortly after. These include the
Noli Me Tangere at the Prado, Madrid, with which it shares that tendency
towards a studied grace expressed in touches of colour and reflected light,
and in the forms and affected poses of the figures.

The luminous landscape answers the brightness that emanates from the
Child and which lights up the whole figure of the Virgin, who is kneeling
with her arms parted in a very expressive gesture of adoration. Yet the
tenderness with which her motherly feeling is conveyed does not detract
from the impressiveness of the divine image, which is even heightened by
the colours of her dress and cloak, brilliant in the miraculous light.

PARMIGIANINO (Francesco Mazzola) (c. 1504–c. 1540)   *Emilian School*
THE MADONNA WITH THE LONG NECK   Panel
Inv. Palatina No. 230   Height 216 cm. (85″)
                                                    Width 132 cm. (52″)

Elena Baiardi, the wife of Francesco Tagliaferri of Parma, commissioned
Parmigianino in 1534 to paint this picture, which was placed in the
Tagliaferri Chapel of Santa Maria dei Servi in 1542. Acquired in 1698
by the Grand Prince of Tuscany Ferdinando de' Medici, son of Grand
Duke Cosimo III, it was taken to the Palazzo Pitti, where it entered the
gallery on Ferdinando's death.

The picture is unfinished, as attested by the Latin inscription on the
platform of the colonnade, before which one sees the small figure of the
prophet Isaiah.

Parmigianino was the representative at Parma of Mannerism—that is,
of those art currents in the second half of the sixteenth century that
continued the tradition of the High Renaissance by developing its themes
in novel ways. He is distinguished chiefly by his peculiar linearism, which
tends towards the 'serpentine form' originating with Michelangelo but
here made more fluid by its derivation from Correggio. This picture is
the most typical product of Parmigianino's Mannerism, with its figures
that are elongated and supple yet not lacking in human warmth.

His refinements of form, stylistic transfigurations of elements from various sources, Tuscan and Emilian, inspire admiration through their very
withdrawal from naturalism as well as from the true classical tradition.

FEDERICO BAROCCIO (1535–1612) *School of the Marches*

PORTRAIT OF FEDERICO D'URBINO AS A NEW-BORN CHILD   Canvas

Inv. Palatina No. 55   Height 60 cm. (23⅝")
Width 73 cm. (28¾")

The picture bears an inscription with the Prince's name and the date 1605. It comes from the Della Rovere inheritance that went to the Grand Duchess Vittoria, the wife of Ferdinando II, and it is one of Baroccio's late works, already mentioned by Baldinucci as among those in the Grand Duchess's possession. Federico Ubaldo was the son of Duke Francesco Maria II della Rovere and had not long succeeded his father as ruler of the dukedom when he died suddenly in 1632. He had married Claudia de' Medici, daughter of Grand Duke Ferdinando I of Tuscany, and she bore him a daughter Vittoria, who later became Ferdinando II's wife.

The theme here has that mark of grace and delicacy found in a great many works by the painter, and it reveals that taste for certain elegances which give his colour a special vivaciousness. An example here is the sumptuous brocaded coverlet over the baby, like that of the Child in the Prado *Nativity*.

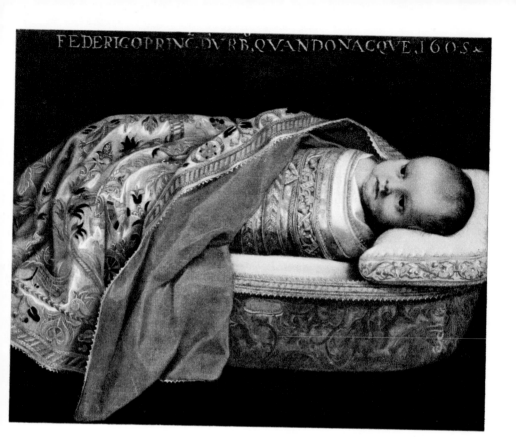
FEDERICO PRINC. DVRB. QVANDO NACQVE. 1605.

ANNIBALE CARRACCI (1560–1609)
A BACCHANTE
Inv. No. 1452

Bolognese School
Canvas
Height 112 cm. (44¹/₈″)
Width 142 cm. (55⁷/₈″)

The picture was bought from Camillo Bolognetti in 1620 by Grand
Duke Cosimo II for 200 ducats. Malvasia (1678) saw it in the grand-
ducal collections, and it is mentioned in the gallery inventory of 1753.
It is an early work and dates from the penultimate decade of the sixteenth century, when the artist was endeavouring chiefly to imitate Titian,
both in composition and in the choice of subjects, and above all in a
tendency towards a painterly richness ill-suited to his Correggio-
dominated training.

Venturi has associated the picture with the *Pluto and Cerberus* in the
Galleria Estense at Modena and the *Vulcan* at Besançon, partly on account
of the strained sculptural effects through which the artist lapses slightly
into academicism; but his Venetian side still prevails in the light, in the
impasting of the colour, in the very lively details, and in a painterly
sensuousness that goes well with the sensuality of the theme.

Despite some heaviness in the forms and hardness in the contours, the
work soon became famous, partly perhaps, owing to the character of its
subject, but just as much because of the highly successful diagonal composition, the unforced naturalism, and the freshness and originality that
Carracci succeeded in giving his creations. At the Pitti there is a painted
sketch for this composition and at the Uffizi a drawing.

CARAVAGGIO *(Michelangelo Merisi)* (1573–1610)   *Italian School*
Young Bacchus   Canvas
Inv. No. 5312   Height 98 cm. (38⁵/₈″)
                                                  Width 85 cm. (33¹/₂″)

This painting, which used to be in the reference section of the Uffizi, was
at first considered an old copy of a lost early Caravaggio, even though the
'amazing tactile values of the fruit and the ornamented dish' were
recognized. However, a cautious cleaning very soon persuaded people
that it was not a copy but an original early work, and indeed one of his
most beautiful, done by the artist round about 1589. This conclusion was
reached less because of the Bacchus's resemblance in type to others by
Caravaggio, than because of the connection between this 'still-life' and
examples from his secure works, of which it repeats the perfection met
in the form no less than in the fascinating brilliant colour, and because
of the contrast of the flesh-tints with the black hair, brows, eyes, and
bow.

   In the bottle the head of a youth whose features recall Caravaggio's
is mirrored very small: it is thus a reflection of the painter, resembling
the image of the *Boy with a Basket of Fruit* at the Galleria Borghese,
which is said to be a self-portrait.

   In spite of some doubt, this painting is recognizable as the one recorded
by Giovanni Baglione in his *Vite dei pittori* (1642) as the first of the
small pictures Caravaggio did at Rome after leaving the Cavalier d'Arpino:
'a Bacchus with some varied bunches of grapes, done very carefully but in
a rather dry manner'.

CRISTOFANO ALLORI (1577–1621)
JUDITH
Inv. Palatina No. 41

Florentine School
Canvas
Height 139 cm. (54³/₄″)
Width 116 cm. (45⁵/₈″)

Baldinucci gives varied information about this picture, telling us that it was painted for Cardinal Alessandro Orsini (elevated to the purple in 1615, as appears from a note on the back of an Allori drawing owned by Michelangelo Buonarroti the Younger), and that Allori 'did in Judith's face a life-like portrait of Mazzafirra', a woman with whom he had fallen in love. We are further informed that 'he painted himself in the picture as Holofernes', after letting his beard grow specially, and that the old woman has the features of Mazzafirra's mother.

This picture, which many consider the finest Florentine work of the seventeenth century, has all the characteristics that made Allori the most esteemed painter at that period and one much sought after by the grandducal family, which as always included several art lovers among its members.

Allori's drawing is particularly delicate, as can be seen from the many studies he made for his compositions, but it is above all the warm colour and perfect blending of the hues that have given his pictures their well-deserved reputation. The vigour and the grandeur of Judith's pose are not diminished by the loving care of the execution; and the correctness of the still sixteenth-century form is not the least reason for the immediate and lasting success of this work.

GUERCINO *(Giovan Francesco Barbieri)* (1591–1666)   *Bolognese School*
THE MADONNA OF THE SWALLOW   Canvas
Inv. Palatina No. 156   Height 118 cm. (46^1/$_2$″)
                                                  Width 88 cm. (34^5/$_8$″)

This is a free but entirely authentic repetition of the Virgin group in
the big *St William of Aquitaine receiving the Cowl*. Considered the artist's
masterpiece, the latter was done in 1620 for the church of the Chierici
Regolari di San Gregorio and is now in the Pinacoteca at Bologna. In
the Pitti variant the figures of St Joseph and St James are missing and
the angel is completely different, even as regards position. Marangoni
has noticed in the Bologna painting a composition of rhomboidal structure
that is given movement by the separate figures, which in their turn are
built on the same plan. The lozenge in which the Virgin is inscribed is
still more apparent in the Pitti canvas, which has retained the characteristic
luminous atmosphere that is the greatest merit of the big composition,
and that puts Guercino among the leading masters of the pictorial revival
in the seventeenth century.

Guercino understood Venetian chiaroscuro as an investigation of depth,
and in thinking about the Venetians he produced original transformations
of his memories, as here of Palma in the Virgin and of Veronese in the
Child.

SALVATORE ROSA (1615–1673)   *Neapolitan School*
SEASCAPE   Canvas
Inv. Palatina No. 4   Height 233 cm. (91³/₄")
                                       Width 399 cm. (157¹/₈")

The picture is signed at the bottom on the left. According to Baldinucci
it was done for Gian Carlo de' Medici, brother of Grand Duke Ferdinando II and later a cardinal, who had got Rosa to come to Florence
and to Rome, where he had made his acquaintance. Currently it was in
the collection of the Grand Prince of Tuscany, Cosimo III's son Ferdinando. It must therefore date from between 1640, the year when Rosa
went to Florence, and 1649, when he returned to Rome. He had then
already acquired that breadth of vision to which his landscapes owe their
fame: the richness of his colour, the luminosity of his airy backgrounds,
and the spirit and life of the incidents introduced into his compositions
account for the success that has attended his work down the centuries.

Rosa was also famous for his battle scenes, and at that period in Italy
he had no competition, apart from Claude Lorrain, in the field of landscape painting. At Naples he had been taught chiefly by Fracanzano; but
what set him on his course as a landscapist was above all examining
Agostino Tassi's pictures in Rome.

ROSALBA CARRIERA (1675–1757)   *Venetian School*
PORTRAIT OF A LADY   Pastel on paper
Inv. No. 3099   Height 47.9 cm. (18⁷/₈″)
                                 Width 33.5 cm. (13¹/₄″)

We do not know which family the woman shown in the pastel belonged to, but it was certainly an aristocratic one, as the fame of this celebrated portraitist spread right from the start, and princes and sovereigns competed to have her depict members of their house. Rosalba's portraits won universal admiration thanks to her matchless ability to render the charm of her sitters through the delicacy and paleness of her colours, which a uniform light softens in their transitions and gradations, attuning them to the pink of the tender skins and to the exquisite refinement of the magnificent silks of the costumes.

It is above all the female portraits that have remained specially famous; but just as successful are those of illustrious people she had the opportunity to paint at Venice, Paris (where she went in 1720), Modena (1723), and Vienna (1730). All bear the personal mark of her style, conveyed particularly well by the pastel technique that she brought to perfection and spread in France and England.

This picture came from the Palazzo della Crocetta at Florence in 1861.

CANALETTO *(Giovanni Antonio)* (1697–1768) *Venetian School*
THE PALAZZO DUCALE AND THE PIAZZETTA Canvas
Inv. No. 1334 Height 68 cm. (26³/₄")
Width 99.5 cm. (39")

Among all the works by this leader of the eighteenth-century Venetian *vedutisti,* this is one of the most notable, for the special sensitivity of the rich colour and for the breadth and freedom in the rapid sketching of the gondolas and gondoliers that enliven the scene imaginatively without reducing its truth as a representation. But what contributes most to Canaletto's charm is the crystal light that dominates his canvases and wraps everything in its purity, the faultless perspective, and the minuteness of the details, which is never carried to excess.

Canaletto has left us an imperishable vision of the many aspects of eighteenth-century Venice, which still kept its prestige and taste for splendour despite financial and political decline; of that Venice which remained, and still remains, a unique city through all the changes wrought by man and time. In this picture, too, which probably dates from about 1730 and thus from before the visits to England, one of the city's most famous views has been transformed into an image that is wholly new and enchanting, thanks to the limpid air that fills the space and the excellent visibility it gives.

The work came from the Villa del Poggio Imperial in 1796.

ROGIER VAN DER WEYDEN (1400–1464)   *Early Netherlandish School*
THE ENTOMBMENT   Panel
Inv. No. 1114   Height 110 cm. (43¼")
                                            Width 96 cm. (37¾")

This picture was once believed to be a work by Dürer, and it passed for one in the collection of Cardinal Carlo de' Medici, son of Ferdinando I and brother of Cosimo II. The Cardinal, who died in 1666, left it as a contribution to the arch-ducal collections. It has been suggested that the panel formed the centre of the polyptych acquired by Leonello d'Este in 1449, which was seen during the same year in the Marquis's study by Giriaco d'Ancona and was described in 1454 by Bartolommeo Facio as well. Nevertheless it should be pointed out that the two figures at the back are not mentioned in Facio's description.

Lassaigne has noted that the picture's layout makes use of a Fra Angelico construction (the one in his *Lamentation* at Munich from the predella of the work for the high altar of San Marco), which Giovanni Bellini was to think out in his turn; but Lassaigne considers the figures to have been combined with the landscape in an arbitrary way, a result of the artist's difficulty in adapting himself to a composition he had not devised himself. In point of fact the placing of the figures around Christ, still in the attitude of one crucified, is exceptional for the Early Netherlandish School, as has already been observed, but it often appears in Italian predellas, from which Rogier may have drawn inspiration. At any rate, the painting must be held to date from the time of the visit to Italy which the artist made for the Jubilee of 1450; and a reflection of this experience may perhaps be seen in the monumentality of the figures, in the balance and architectonic symmetry of the main group, and in the sculpturesque figure of the Magdalen.

HUGO VAN DER GOES (after 1440–1482)   *Early Netherlandish School*
THE PORTINARI ALTARPIECE
Inv. Nos. 3191, 3192, 3193.

Central Panel   Height 253 cm. (99⅝″)
Width 304 cm. (119⅝″)

In the central panel this triptych presents the *Adoration of the Shepherds*.
Executed at Ghent, probably during 1473/1475, for the Medici bank's
agent in Bruges, Tommaso Portinari, the work was sent to Florence to be
placed on the high altar in the church of Sant' Egidio, which belongs to
the hospital of Santa Maria Nuova, founded in 1285 by the purchaser's
ancestor Folco Portinari. It must in any case have been finished before
1478, the year when the painter entered a monastery, and have reached
Florence before 1485, the date of the Ghirlandaio painting in which the
shepherds clearly show the influence of Hugo's work. Lodovico Guicciar-
dini mentions the altarpiece in his *Descrizione di tutti i Paesi Bassi* (1567)
and, before him, Vasari in the first edition of his *Lives* (1550). This
painting is among the most important of the Early Netherlandish School,
owing to the grandeur of the scene and its eminent stylistic qualities. The
representation of the Nativity is enriched by the incidents inserted in the
landscape background: the flight into Egypt, the announcement to the
shepherds, and the arrival of the kings. The whole scene is arranged to
make its separate elements gravitate towards the luminous centre formed
by the Child. These figures are monumental not only in their clothing
and attitudes but in the gravity of their expressions as they take part in
the great event; the way the thickness of the materials is rendered and
the realism of some figures certainly taken from contemporary models do
not detract from the grandeur of the whole. The brightness of the
colours, culminating in the blue of the Virgin's robe, and the strength of
the light that makes the whole scene visible give the work an individual
vividness, which accounts for the tremendous impact it made on the Florentine world of the period. The novelty of the message that arrived from
Flanders, which had of course already sent others less unusual and enduring,
left its mark on many of the artists–even some of the greatest–who during
the last decades of the fifteenth century continued the glorious tradition of
the Florentine Renaissance.

The importance of this triptych also lies in its being the artist's only
certain work, so that it has formed a basis for reconstructing his personality through the identification of his other paintings.

The altarpiece came to the Uffizi in 1900.

HANS MEMLING (c. 1430–1494)   *Early Netherlandish School*

THE MADONNA ENTHRONED BETWEEN TWO ANGELS   Panel

Inv. No. 1024   Height 57 cm. (22$^1/_2$")

Width 43 cm. (16$^7/_8$")

This work was acquired in 1779 from the collection left by the painter Ignazio Hugford. Probably a pupil of Rogier van der Weyden's, Memling did not remain indifferent in his late period to fifteenth-century decorative elegance, and he adorned some of his Madonna pictures with motifs taken from Italian art—interpretations of Paduan or Venetian models. In this example at the Uffizi we accordingly see festoons of leaves, fruit, and flowers held by putti, as in the Vienna *Virgin Enthroned* and in the *Resurrection* triptych at the Louvre.

It has been suggested that this work dates from between 1485 and 1490. Other features too, however, reveal the influence of the Italian Renaissance on Memling. This applies above all to that classic regularity towards which his style constantly tends, especially in the landscapes on to which his pictures open—pictures that are wholly calm and orderly in their natural as well as their architectural elements. This regularity which is also present in the meditative look of the figures, in their poses, in the subtle harmony of the colours, is the artist's most effective means of heightening the spiritual significance of his image.

PETER PAUL RUBENS (1577–1640) *Flemish School*
THE ARTIST WITH HIS BROTHER PHILIP, JUSTUS LIPSIUS,
AND JAN WOUVER (The Four Philosophers) Panel
Inv. Palatina No. 85 Height 164 cm. (64⁵/₈″)
Width 139 cm. (54³/₄″)

The artist is seen standing, first on the left; then come Philip Rubens, Justus Lipsius, and Jan Wouver—the two pupils on either side of their teacher, a distinguished philologist and philosopher. Rubens and his brother met Wouver at Verona in 1602, so the picture could date from that year or slightly later, unless, as some claim, the painter did it in 1608 soon after returning to Antwerp, in memory of his brother, who had recently died. Others actually assign it to the second decade of the century, but the fact that Lipsius died in 1606 makes a date not later than this more likely. The marble bust in the niche is the one believed then to represent Seneca (whose works Lipsius had edited) but now considered that of a Hellenistic poet. It cannot be identified with the herm-type bust at the Uffizi (No. 310), which comes from the Villa Medici, because of the difference in form.

At all events, the picture shows the personality of the artist, aged thirty or just over, already fully developed. It has his wonderful spontaneity, his sensuous and joyful colour, and that characteristic interpretation of his subject which makes him one of the foremost portrait painters of his time: so great is the vivacity and freshness of the images and the power of psychological penetration, not to be found in some of his other portraits, which here effectively renders the master's conversation with his favourite pupils despite the exuberant boldness of the artist's brush.

PETER PAUL RUBENS (1577–1640)　　　　　*Flemish School*
PEASANTS RETURNING FROM THE FIELDS　　　　　Panel
Inv. Palatina No. 14　　　　　Height 121 cm. (47⁵/₈″)
　　　　　Width 194 cm. (76³/₈″)

This picture came from the Duc de Richelieu's collection together with
the one showing Ulysses on the island of the Phaeacians, now also at the
Pitti. It is among the finest examples of landscape painting Rubens has
left us, partly owing to the complete ascendancy of the landscape over
the figures, which animate it in an attractive way but with complete
unity. The beauty of nature is rendered with the artist's own particular
zest, which had led him ever since his early works to observe the details
keenly and achieve an accomplished execution. The city visible in the
background could be Malines, and, if so, it would be reasonable to assign
these pictures to the last years of Rubens' life, when he bought a country-
house in that neighbourhood. All the same, one should remember that
just as effective observations of landscape are also present in works from
the painter's best period, round about 1620. Anyway, the landscape must
be regarded as being entirely by Rubens and not, as some have claimed,
by Lucas van Uden, one of his collaborators. This is convincingly shown
by, among other things, the strongly poetic effect of the colour in the
landscape as well as the figures, which makes this one of the artist's most
admired pictures, its whole composition expressing a calm yet majestic
peace.

PETER PAUL RUBENS (1577–1640)   *Flemish School*
ALLEGORY OF WAR   Canvas
Inv. Palatina No. 86   Height 206 cm. (81¹/₈")
                                                  Width 345 cm. (135⁷/₈")

Rubens himself in 1638 sent this canvas to the painter Justus Sustermans who was eager to have a work of his. The heirs of Sustermans parted with it to the Grand Prince of Tuscany, Cosimo III's son Ferdinando, who was among the most discerning of collectors. In his letter announcing the despatch of the picture, Rubens explains the subject he has treated, inspired by Lucretius and Virgil. The principal figure is Mars, who, having left the Temple of Janus open, threatens the people with ruin and pays no heed to the efforts Venus is making to restrain him. From the other side, he is dragged along by a Fury, whose companions are Pestilence and Famine. On the ground lie Concord with a broken lute, a frightened mother with her weeping child, and an architect with his instruments. The woman in despair is Europe rent by the war. An indisputably clear allegorical composition, it has given Rubens the chance to produce one of his last masterpieces, in this wonderful tangle of forms and colours ruled by a creative mind of incredible fertility and peerless imaginative power. Moreover, the rhythm of the composition is fully suited to the meaning of the scene. During this final period of his life the artist paints for the joy of creating and brings the forms to life in a limpid atmosphere.

ANTHONY VAN DYCK (1599–1641)

PORTRAIT OF CARDINAL GUIDO BENTIVOGLIO

Inv. Palatina No. 82

Flemish School

Canvas

Height 195 cm. (76³/₄″)

Width 147 cm. (57⁷/₈″)

This portrait was painted in Rome in 1623/25, during the artist's second visit. He was then a guest of Bentivoglio, who, having been Papal Nuncio in Flanders and written *Della guerra di Flandra,* patronized Flemish artists. The Cardinal himself—he died in 1644—gave the picture at an unknown date to Grand Duke Ferdinando II de' Medici, who consigned it to the repository on 24 January 1652, and had it placed in the Tribuna of the Uffizi. Bellori, who published his *Vite dei pittori* in 1672, confirms that it was 'at Florence in the Grand Duke's palace'.

As a portraitist Van Dyck only partly derives from Rubens; in actual fact he gave his likenesses a personal imprint of elegance and simplicity, which came to him from his contact with Italian culture, even when their courtly character just required impressiveness. Like the others painted at Rome—of Francesco Colonna (Rome) and Marchesa Spinola (Berlin)—this image of Cardinal Bentivoglio is among his most remarkable portraits, thanks to the breadth of its composition and the restraint of its colour-scheme, which, a play of whites and reds, is also referable to his contact with Italian painting. Its spareness and vigour do not appear again in the later portraits: the whole figure exhales a determination and energy unusual in Van Dyck. The movement and life imparted especially by the pose of the head, which is turned in the opposite direction to the body, make this one of the most successful psychological portraits done anywhere in Europe during the seventeenth century.

ANTHONY VAN DYCK (1599–1641)　　　　　　*Flemish School*
SACRED ALLEGORY　　　　　　　　　　　　　　　　Canvas
Inv. Palatina No. 1105　　　　　　　　Height 73 cm. (28³/₄″)
　　　　　　　　　　　　　　　　　　　　Width 54 cm. (21¹/₄″)

This is an imitation bas-relief in monochrome representing a painted cloth
held up by some angels and fastened at the corners. On the cloth the Virgin
with the Child in her arms is shown standing on a dragon between two
more angels, who bear a crown and a palm. God appears above, and
below there is an inscription shield.

The sword symbolizes the sorrows of Mary, prophesied by Simeon: 'Yea,
a sword shall pierce through thy own soul also, that the thoughts of many
hearts may be revealed.'

The picture seems to have been in Archduke Leopold Wilhelm of
Austria's collection in 1659, but attributed to Abraham van Diepenbeek,
a pupil of Rubens who painted religious subjects, generally in Baroque
stone niches. It came to Florence from the Imperial gallery at Vienna in
1793 on the occasion of an exchange of pictures that yielded, among
others, a Titian Madonna, Dürer's *Adoration of the Magi*, and Giovanni
Bellini's *Sacred Allegory*.

ALBRECHT DÜRER (1471–1528)　　　　　　　*German School*
THE ADORATION OF THE MAGI　　　　　　　　**Panel**
Inv. No. 1434　　　　　　　　　　　　Height 95.5 cm. (37⁵/₈″)
　　　　　　　　　　　　　　　　　　　Width 114 cm. (44⁷/₈″)

This picture bears Dürer's monogram and the date 1504. It was thus completed by the artist at the beginning of his second journey to Italy, very probably while he was staying at Trent. Indeed, it is thought to have been painted for the chapel of the Castello del Buonconsiglio there. It is a mature work, with perhaps excessive attention to detail; but the design of the main group is simple, informal, and full of loving intimacy. The intentional realism of the figures, including the animals, compliments the skilful perspective effects of the architecture. There is a possible reflection of the visit to Italy only in the wooded hill in the background, which could recall one of the Tridentine landscapes drawn by Dürer. The colour is brilliant and enamel-like, and the artist has enjoyed stressing the costliness of certain objects, while revealing the more lyrical tendency that one meets in his works from these years. His engraving of the *Adoration of the Magi* has a similar layout.

The picture was one in the Imperial gallery at Vienna and came to the Uffizi in 1793 in exchange for other paintings.

ALBRECHT ALTDORFER (c. 1480–1538)   *German School*
THE DEPARTURE OF ST FLORIAN   Panel
Inv. Depositi No. 5   Height 81.4 cm. (32")
Width 67 cm. (26³/₈")

The panel was once in the possession of the Spannocchi family at Siena.
It belongs to a series of scenes from the life of St Florian painted round
about 1518 for the church of St Florian near Linz, and it bears the
artist's monogram.

Though his early works do not show many traces of Dürer's style,
Altdorfer sometimes drew inspiration from his themes. Then, after being
noticeably influenced by Cranach, he achieved a highly emotional style
of his own and unity in his compositions. His art ended by reflecting
above all the influence of Michael Pacher's St Wolfgang Altarpiece,
which enabled him to arrive at the breadth of form and grandeur of
design found in the big polyptych for St Florian, whose parts are now
dispersed in various European galleries: two panels at the Uffizi, three at
the Germanisches Nationalmuseum, Nuremberg, and others elsewhere.

During his late period Altdorfer is distinguished by the increased
plasticity of his figures and by the breadth of vision in his landscapes,
to which he tends to give more and more importance.

LUCAS CRANACH THE ELDER (1472–1553)　　　German School
ADAM　　　　　　　　　　　　　　　　　　　　　　　Panel
Inv. No. 1459　　　　　　　　　　　　Height 172 cm. (67³/₄")
　　　　　　　　　　　　　　　　　　　Width 63 cm. (24³/₄")

EVE
Inv. No. 1458　　　　　　　　　　　　Height 167 cm. (65³/₄")
　　　　　　　　　　　　　　　　　　　Width 61 cm. (24")

The *Adam* bears Cranach's monogram and the date 1528. Both panels are only documented as being in the Uffizi from 1704. The last representative of Gothic realism in Germany, Cranach was anti-Renaissance and at first came under Dürer's influence, as is still shown by these pictures. But in his nudes he also retains the arabesque of Gothic line at the expense of all the possible plastic qualities of such images. His colours derive from Gothic miniature painting but are interpreted in a fanciful way and go well with the mannered grace of his figures. He is a better portraitist, especially in the highly expressive likenesses of his early period. Later his portraits also have a certain depth of psychological insight and considerable vitality, and in any case one must recognize the distinctive character of his untrammeled creative imagination, which has brought his pictures such success ever since he painted them.

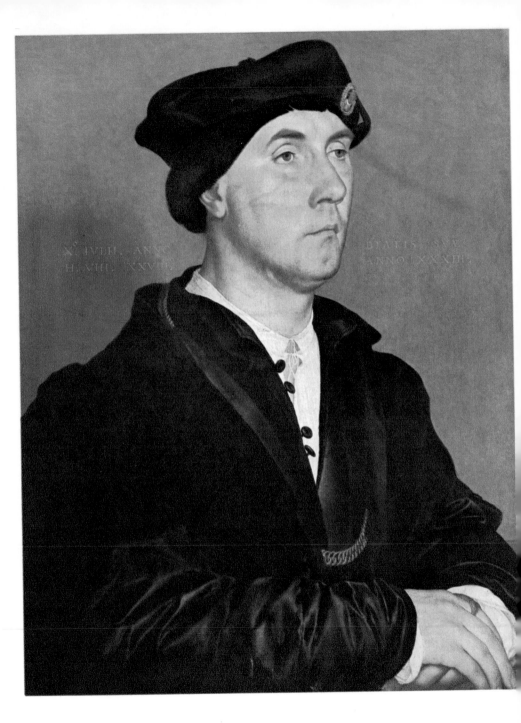

HANS HOLBEIN THE YOUNGER (1497–1543) *German School*
SIR RICHARD SOUTHWELL   Panel

Inv. No. 1087   Height 47.5 cm. (18³/₄")

Width 38 cm. (15")

The portrait was painted in 1536 and presented to Cosimo II de' Medici by Thomas Howard, Earl of Arundel, in 1621. Baldinucci mentions it as being in the Tribuna of the Uffizi. Southwell was one of Henry VIII's Privy Councillors and an ancestor of Elizabeth Southwell, whose husband was in the Grand Duke's service in Florence. The picture belongs to the period of the artist's second stay in London, which lasted from 1532 till 1543, the year of his death, and yielded an especially rich crop of portraits, mostly showing members of the court of Henry VIII, whose official painter Holbein had become.

In the portraits from this period, with their breadth of conception and accurately rendered settings, we undoubtedly have examples of the artist's best style. They are stately portraits, ceremonial ones, and biographical in the sixteenth-century sense. Powerful and very lively, they achieve a perfection of style and technique, and sometimes also a depth of psychological insight, such as to recreate before us the sitter's physical form.

Holbein was able to comprehend the very essence of the Italian Renaissance and to interpret it with originality in classically monumental compositions.

DIEGO RODRÍGUEZ DE SILVA Y VELÁZQUEZ (1599–1660)

Spanish School

Portrait of Philip IV of Spain

Inv. Palatina No. 243

Canvas

Height 126 cm. (49⁵/₈")

Width 93 cm. (36⁵/₈")

This, it is claimed, is one of the two portraits of Philip IV that Baldinucci says were sent to Pietro Tacca to help him when he was modelling his equestrian statue of the King; Baldinucci, however, ascribes both the works he mentions to Rubens. Today the prevailing view is that this likeness really is one of those sent to Tacca, although some consider it a copy specially done in Velázquez' studio of the equestrian portrait of 1636, now at the Prado. The quality of the Pitti work is such that it certainly cannot be excluded from the painter's *œuvre*. In it one can see the direct influence of Titian, with whose work Velázquez was already familiar at the Spanish court, and of Venetian painting generally, which he got to know during his travels in Italy.

BARTOLOMÉ ESTEBAN MURILLO (1617–1682) *Spanish School*
THE MADONNA OF THE ROSARY Canvas
Inv. Palatina No. 56 Height 165 cm. (65")
Width 109 cm. (42⁷/₈")

Murillo repeated this subject several times. There are versions at the Louvre, at Dresden, and in the Wallace Collection, London, the last being a school work. According to the Dresden catalogue the Virgin is a portrait of Doña Maria de Leganés.

Even if indirectly, Murillo is an Italianizing artist, his qualities being facility, naturalness, soft modelling, and especially airy lightness and transparency. Through these he has given in his painting, which is all harmony and delicateness, full expression to his devout nature.

The picture was bought by Grand Duke Ferdinando III in 1822 from the painter Fedele Acciai for 900 scudi.

JAN MIENZE MOLENAER (c. 1610–1668)   *Dutch School*
PEASANTS IN A TAVERN   Panel
Inv. No. 1278   Height 69.5 cm. (27³/₈″)
                                         Width 115 cm. (45¹/₄″)

A pupil of Frans Hals, Molenaer is among the greatest Dutch genre
painters of the seventeenth century. His early works derive from those
of his teacher. He lived first at Haarlem, then at Amsterdam, returning
to his birthplace during his late period, to which this picture, with its
fluent, broad handling, presumably belongs. His last works bring him
close to Adriaen van Ostade.

The Uffizi painting was first ascribed to Adriaen Brouwer, but a recent
restoration uncovered Molenaer's signature. It came from the grand-
ducal repository in 1770.

HERCULES PIETERSZ SEGHERS (c. 1590–1640)　　　*Dutch School*

LANDSCAPE　　　　　　　　　　　　　　　　　　Panel

Inv. No. 1303　　　　　　　　　　　　Height 55 cm. (21⁵/₈″)

　　　　　　　　　　　　　　　　　　　Width 100 cm. (39³/₈″)

This work was presented as a Rembrandt to the Uffizi in 1839 by Baroness Maria Hadfield Cosway. Wilhelm von Bode attributed it to its true author. The landscape does in fact show Seghers to be a precursor of Rembrandt: it is the execution and the drawing of the small figures that invalidate the first attribution. His etchings and his signed landscape at Berlin serve as a point of departure for reconstructing the *œuvre* of this painter whose paintings are extremely rare and who was discovered at the beginning of our century. Here, too, in what is considered his masterpiece, he presents an extremely individual style, as he has depicted his landscape without any concern for objectivity. Instead, he has sought to convey, with a few light notes of colour, the feelings that nature awakened in him, giving the impression that things are seen from a long way off, in a remote silence. The dramatic grandeur of this picture relates it to the *Landscape* at the Museum Boymans-Vanbeunigen and another in a Dutch private collection, which are datable to between 1620 and 1627.

At a certain period Rembrandt clearly drew inspiration from Seghers' landscapes, and it has been suggested that the Uffizi example is one of the eight works by him that Rembrandt once owned.

REMBRANDT VAN RIJN (1606–1669)　　　　　*Dutch School*
SELF-PORTRAIT AS A YOUNG MAN　　　　　　　Canvas
Inv. No. 3890　　　　　　　　　　　　Height 61 cm. (24″)
　　　　　　　　　　　　　　　　　　Width 52 cm. (20¹/₂″)

It has been suggested that in this and other early self-portraits of the
artist done at a time when he had already grown in fame, ability, and
self-assurance, one should see not only his desire to study his own features
but also a little vanity, almost narcissism. The first self-portraits belong
to the years round about 1630, even before Rembrandt had settled at
Amsterdam. This one at the Uffizi must, however, date from after his
move to Amsterdam, and it shows precisely that self-confidence which
his by then assured success had helped to give him, after the famous
Anatomy Lesson, in spite of the defiant look that is the most fascinating
element in the painting.

At the Uffizi there are two other impressive self-portraits of Rembrandt,
but they come from his late period and reflect the state of humiliation to
which he had been reduced after all his domestic and financial misfortunes.
One of these was acquired by Cardinal Leopoldo de' Medici, whereas the
early likeness was in the collection of the Marchesi Gerini at Florence
in 1724, and was purchased in 1818 by Grand Duke Ferdinando III of
Lorraine.

REMBRANDT VAN RIJN (1606–1669)   *Dutch School*
PORTRAIT OF AN OLD MAN   Canvas
Inv. No. 8435   Height 102 cm. (40⅛")
                                            Width 73 cm. (28¾")

This painting is signed and bears a date that cannot now be read with certainty; perhaps 1666. It was probably obtained at Amsterdam by Cosimo de' Medici (afterwards Cosimo III) during a visit to Holland in 1667. Then it passed into the collection of his son Ferdinando, Grand Prince of Tuscany, from which it entered the gallery in 1698. It has also been suggested that it was acquired by Cardinal Leopoldo de' Medici, but this theory is less convincing.

J. Zwarts believed the portrait represented Haham Saul Levy Morteyra (died 1665), who was Chief Rabbi of the Portuguese Jews in Amsterdam from 1616 to 1660 and stood by Rembrandt for twenty-five years. This identification is plausible on account of the painter's close ties with various members of the Hispano-Portuguese synagogue at Amsterdam, but not enough evidence exists to confirm it. This is one of the most striking portraits from the period round about 1650–60. Everything is firmly constructed, despite the form that is not always fully defined and the directness of handling that leads Rembrandt to alternate rapid light strokes with long dark ones. In the chiaroscuro resulting from this lies the whole of the picture's play of colour.

A work in the artist's late style, it is among those that testify most fully to the vigour and vitality of his genius and the assurance of his technique, even during these years when his life was drawing to a close in the affliction of solitude and penury.

JACOB VAN RUISDAEL (1628–1682)   *Dutch School*
LANDSCAPE   Canvas
Inv. No. 1201   Height 52 cm. (20^1/$_2$″)
                                            Width 60 cm. (23^5/$_8$″)

Ruisdael is among the greatest Dutch landscape artists of the seventeenth century. His views of woods and dunes around Haarlem, where he began his career, have been conceived and painted with breadth and vigour, but they still show a trace of sadness that in no way detracts from the majesty of their structure. Endowed with a remarkable decorative sense, he succeeded in fixing on his canvas the memory of his affectionate observations of nature, rendering perfectly the tints and shades of the vegetation and enveloping everything in a wonderful light. His meticulous execution does not reduce the solidity of the volumes. Here, the feeling of the storm is in the sun as it peeps out wanly from between the clouds and makes the foliage of the wind-shaken trees glitter, while, to the right, the grassland gives back a cold light.

The painting is signed on the right. It was acquired in 1797 by Count de Gallifet and entered the Uffizi the following year.

GODFRIED SCHALCKEN (1643–1706)
Girl with a Candle
Inv. No. 1118

Dutch School
Canvas
Height 61 cm. (24")
Width 50 cm. (19⁵/₈")

Schalcken belongs to the school that spread out mainly from Leyden and excelled in painting small genre pictures. In this one the principal effect is that of the candle lighting up the girl's pretty face as she shields it with her right hand. The artist had been taught by Samuel van Hoogstraten at Dordrecht and by Gerard Dou at Leyden. In 1691 he joined the painters guild at The Hague, where he died in 1706.

The picture is signed. There is one with a similar subject at the Musées Royaux des Beaux-Arts, Brussels. The Uffizi's came to the gallery in 1773 from the Medici Villa at Poggio a Caiano.

NICOLAS FROMENT (Mentioned 1461–1476)   *French School*
THE RAISING OF LAZARUS   Panel
Inv. No. 1065

Central Panel	Height 175 cm. (68⁷/₈″)	

Central Panel   Height 175 cm. (68$^7/_8$″)
     Width 134 cm. (52$^3/_4$″)
Wings   Height 175 cm. (68$^7/_8$″)
     Width 66 cm. (26″)

In the middle this triptych portrays the *Raising of Lazarus*. Its left wing shows *Martha kneeling before Christ* and, on the outside, a *Madonna and Child;* its right *St Mary Magdalen annointing Christ's Feet* and, on the outside, portraits of the donors.

Signed and dated 1461, the work appears to have been given by Cosimo the Elder to the church of the Bosco ai Frati friary in the Mugello, and it remained there till Napoleon's suppression of the religious houses in 1808–10. It is not to be thought, however, that Cosimo commissioned the triptych, since the chief donor is in ecclesiastical dress, but rather that he may have acquired it through one of the agents of his bank in France. Froment is an artist who, with his other certain work—the *Burning Bush* —as well, had a considerable effect not only on Provençal painting of the period but also on that of northern France. Though the presence of an Hispano-Moorish jar is quite usual in pictures from Provence, this does not rule out the possibility that the work was executed in Italy. The dominant influence in Froment is Flemish; and Avignon, then a great centre of European painting, saw other masters flourish at his side.

This *Raising of Lazarus* is his most important work, and it shows that International Gothic art persisted at a time when it had been completely vanquished in Italy by the Renaissance. The main thing to note is the decorative sense apparent not just in the triptych's form but more especially in the almost miniature-like distribution of the colour. It achieves remarkable vivacity and freshness in the landscape backgrounds of the wing panels.

FRANÇOIS CLOUET (c. 1516/20–1572)   *French School*
PORTRAIT OF FRANCIS I, KING OF FRANCE   Panel
Inv. No. 987   Height 27.5 cm. (10⁷/₈")
     Width 22.5 cm. (8⁷/₈")

The artist was Jean Clouet's son and he continued the style of his father, who is known mainly as a portraitist through a group of drawings in the Musée Condé at Chantilly. François, however, did not achieve the same delicacy of colouring or sensitivity in depicting the human face. His works are very rare and this is undoubtedly among the best, on account of the elegant drawing and a colour harmony that has made some critics ascribe it to a follower of Jean Clouet. De Laborde, indeed, suggests that it was by Jean himself, and so do many others; but the king's age in the portrait rules out his attribution. If the picture really is by François, it must belong to this early period, as Francis I died in 1547.

The almost miniaturist refinement of execution makes up for the conventionality of the composition, which derives from one of the Chantilly drawings mentioned above.

CLAUDE LORRAIN *(Claude Gellée)* (1600–1682)   *French School*
A SEAPORT AT SUNSET   Canvas
Inv. No. 1096   Height 102 cm. (40¹/₈")
                                                  Width 133 cm. (52¹/₈")

This painting comes from the collection left by Cardinal Leopoldo de'
Medici, and it has been in the gallery since 1773. Baldinucci is referring
to it when he says that 'for Cardinal de' Medici he did [a picture]
in which he painted the palace of the Serenissima Casa at Trinità de'
Monti, and a very lovely view of the sea'. In his *Liber veritatis*, where
he kept a record of all his own works, Claude himself says it was executed
for a Cardinal de' Medici. As the work is signed and dated 1637, one
must conclude that the cardinal was Grand Duke Ferdinando II's uncle,
Carlo de' Medici, the only member of the family belonging to the Sacred
College at that time. This is the finest and best known of the *Seaports*
Claude painted during these years, in which he recreates reality by freely
interpreting the things he sees and enveloping them in the remarkable
atmosphere that is vital to his art. The amazing effects of the sunbeams
mirrored in the sea make the whole luminous stage vibrate miraculously,
and they form the most poetic element of the entire composition. In this
picture Claude really is the painter of light and sun, here rendered at
his favourite hour—the hour of sunset—which yields those golden tones
that delight him.

ANTOINE WATTEAU (1684–1721)
THE FLUTE-PLAYER
Inv. No. 990

French School
Canvas
Height 36.5 cm. (14³/₈″)
Width 46 cm. (18¹/₈″)

This is among the most attractive products of Watteau's second style, a work by the greatest representative of French painting of the eighteenth century, which has marked it with its aristocratic elegance. Lively drawing, fresh colour, and a love of theatrical subjects in which the artist's poetic temperament has found a way of living out its dreams, are the main features of an *œuvre* that culminates in the series of *Fêtes galantes*, all masterpieces, which give first place to music and dancing, the focus of his passions.

Certainly authentic, this work is especially notable as an example of Watteau the colourist, with his natural ingenuousness and his very delicate intuition. During this second period, which produced compositions with small figures, even the staging of the scene always has something fanciful about it that recalls the theatre.

The picture came from the formerly grand-ducal repository in 1860.

ITALIAN SCHOOLS OF THE THIRTEENTH
AND FOURTEENTH CENTURIES

Meliore di Jacopo
The Saviour, the Virgin and Saints

Pietro Lorenzetti The Beata Umiltà

Ambrogio Lorenzetti The Presentation in the Temple

Bernardo Daddi
The Virgin and Child between SS Matthew and Nicholas

Jacopo del Casentino
The Coronation of the Virgin

Giovanni da Milano Saints and Martyrs

Master of St Cecilia
Scenes from the Life of St Cecilia

Gherardo Starnina The Thebaid

Lorenzo Monaco Scene from the Life of St Benedict

Lorenzo Monaco Scene from the Life of St Benedict

Lorenzo Monaco Scene from the Life of St Benedict

Lorenzo Monaco Scene from the Life of St Benedict

Lorenzo Monaco Scene from the Life of St Benedict

Lorenzo Monaco Scene from the Life of St Benedict

274

ITALIAN SCHOOL OF THE FIFTEENTH CENTURY

Piero della Francesca
Allegorical Triumphs of the Duke and Duchess of Urbino

Vecchietta The Madonna and Child with Saints

Domenico Veneziano
The Madonna and Child with Saints

Fra Angelico
Madonna and Child

Jacopo Bellini Madonna and Child

Piero del Pollaiuolo Charity

Benozzo Gozzoli The Mystic Marriage of St Catherine

Benozzo Gozzoli Two Saints

Benozzo Gozzoli Pietà

Antonio and Piero del Pollaiuolo
Altarpiece of the Three Saints

Antonio del Pollaiuolo
Hercules and the Hydra   Hercules and Antaeus

Antonio del Pollaiuolo
Portrait of Galeazzo Maria Sforza

Piero del Pollaiuolo
St Jerome

Andrea Mantegna
The Madonna of the Caves

Andrea Mantegna
Portrait of a member of the Gonzaga Family

Cosimo Tura
St Dominic

Francesco Botticini The Three Archangels

Sandro Botticelli The Annunciation

Sandro Botticelli
St Augustine in his Cell

Sandro Botticelli
The Discovery of the Murder of Holophernes

Sandro Botticelli
Fortitude

277

Sandro Botticelli
The Madonna of the Pomegranate

Sandro Botticelli
The Madonna of the Magnificat

Sandro Botticelli The Resurrection

Sandro Botticelli
St Augustine and a Child on the Seashore

Sandro Botticelli
Salome with the Head of the Baptist

Sandro Botticelli
The Extraction of the Heart of Bishop Ignatius

Sandro Botticelli
Portrait of a young Man

Sandro Botticelli
Portrait of a young Woman

Antoniazzo Romano
Virgin and Child

Giorgione The Judgment of Salomon

Filippino Lippi
The Virgin in Adoration

Filippino Lippi Self-Portrait

Filippino Lippi Portrait of an Old Man

Filippino Lippi The Death of Lucrece

Giovanni Bellini The Lamentation over the Dead Christ

Mariotto Albertinelli The Annunciation

Mariotto Albertinelli The Nativity

Mariotto Albertinelli
The Presentation in the Temple

Piero di Cosimo The Immaculate Conception

Bernardino de' Conti Portrait of a Man

Giovanni Antonio Boltraffio Narcissus at the Fountain

Luca Signorelli An Allegory of Fecundity

Luca Signorelli
The Madonna and Child

Luca Signorelli
The Holy Family

Luca Signorelli
The Crucifixion with the Magdalen

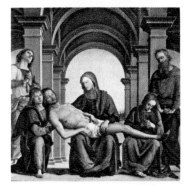

Pietro Perugino
Mary Magdalen

Pietro Perugino The Deposition

Pietro Perugino
Portrait of Francesco delle Opere

Pietro Perugino The Entombment

Pietro Perugino Madonna del Sacco

ITALIAN SCHOOL OF THE SIXTEENTH CENTURY

Raphael La Gravida

Raphael
Portrait of Tommaso Inghirami

Raphael
Portrait of Maddalena Doni

Raphael Julius II

Raphael The Vision of Ezekiel

Raphael
Portrait of Cardinal Dovizzi

Raphael
The Madonna of the Window

Domenico Puligo
Portrait of Pietro Carnesecchi

Lodovico Mazzolino The Massacre of the Innocents

Palma Vecchio
The Holy Family with SS John and Magdalen

Andrea del Sarto
The Assumption of the Virgin

Andrea del Sarto
The Assumption of the Virgin

Andrea del Sarto The Entombment

Andrea del Sarto The Story of Joseph

Andrea del Sarto The Story of Joseph

Andrea del Sarto The Annunciation

Andrea del Sarto
St John the Baptist

Andrea del Sarto
Portrait of a young Woman

Andrea del Sarto
The Madonna of the Harpies

Palmezzano The Crucifixion

Ridolfo del Ghirlandaio
Portrait of a young Woman

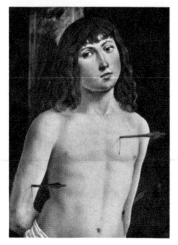

Lorenzo Costa St Sebastian

Lorenzo Costa Portrait of Giovanni II Bentivoglio

Dosso Dossi Nymph pursued by a Satyr

Dosso Dossi Rest in Flight

Dosso Dossi Sorcery

Dosso Dossi Portrait of a Warrior

Giovanni Girolamo Savoldo
The Transfiguration

Sodoma St Sebastian

Girolamo Genga St Sebastian

285

Domenico Beccafumi The Holy Family

Garofalo The Gipsy

Cecchino Salviati The Three Fates

Paris Bordone Portrait **of a** Woman

Giovanni Battista Moroni
Portrait of Count Secco-Suardi

Giovanni Battista Moroni
Portrait of a Man

Giulio Campi The Guitar-Player

Girolamo Romanino Portrait of a Boy

Jacopo Bassano Hunting Dogs

Leandro Bassano Family Concert

Bachiacca Scene from the Life of St Acacius

Bachiacca
The Archangel Raphael and the young Tobias

Rosso Fiorentino
Portrait of a young Girl

Rosso Fiorentino The Madonna
in Majesty surrounded by Saints

Pontormo The Madonna and Child
between SS Jerome and Francis

287

Pontormo St Anthony

Pontormo
The Virgin and Child with the Infant St John

Pontormo Portrait of a Man

Pontormo
Portrait of a Woman with a Basket of Spindles

Pontormo
Portrait of the Musician Francesco dell' Ajolle

Pontormo The Martyrdom of the Eleven Thousand

Bronzino
Portrait of Bartolommeo Panciatichi

Bronzino
Portrait of Lucrezia Panciatichi

Bronzino
Portrait of a young Girl with a Book

Bronzino
Portrait of a Medicean Princess

Bronzino
Portrait of Maria de' Medici

Bronzino
Portrait of the Engineer Luca Martini

Bronzino
Portrait of Guidobaldo della Rovere

Bronzino The Holy Family

Bronzino
Portrait of Cosimo I de' Medici in Armour

289

Titian A Knight of Malta

Titian The Saviour

Titian Francesco Maria della Rovere,
Duke of Urbino

Titian Portrait of Cardinal
Ippolito de' Medici

Titian Portrait of Andrea Vesalio

Titian Portrait of Tommaso Mosti

Venetian School Portrait of a Man

Sebastiano del Piombo The Martyrdom of St Agatha

Sebastiano del Piombo
Portrait of Baccio Valori

Tintoretto
Portrait of Luigi Cornaro

Tintoretto
Portrait of Vincenzo Zeno

Tintoretto
Portrait of an Old Man in a Fur Coat

Tintoretto Christ at the Well

Tintoretto The Samaritan Woman

291

Tintoretto Portrait of an Admiral

Correggio Rest in Flight

Correggio The Virgin in Glory

Parmigianino
The Madonna of St Zachariah

Veronese Portrait of a Man

Veronese St Agatha

Baroccio
The Madonna del Popolo

Baroccio
Jesus appearing to St Mary Magdalen

Baroccio
Portrait of Francesco Maria della Rovere

Caravaggio Head of Medusa

ITALIAN SCHOOL OF THE SEVENTEENTH CENTURY

Scarsellino The Judgment of Paris

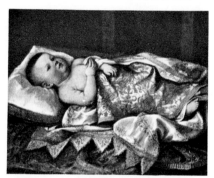

Tiberio Titi Leopoldo de' Medici as a Child

Palma Giovane St Margaret

Cerano Sacra Conversazione

Tiberio Tinelli Portrait of a Man

Giovanni da San Giovanni
The Priest Arlotto

Artemisia Gentileschi Judith

Matteo Rosselli The Triumph of David

Guercino Summer Diversions

Cavallino Esther and Ahasuerus

Guido Reni Young Bacchus

Guido Reni Cleopatra

Salvatore Rosa
Landscape with Ruins and a Bridge

Salvatore Rosa Seascape

Salvatore Rosa Self-Portrait

ITALIAN SCHOOL OF THE EIGHTEENTH CENTURY

Piazzetta Susanna and the Elders

Crespi The Fair at Poggio a Caiano

Crespi The Flea

Baciccio
Portrait of Cardinal Leopoldo de' Medici

Magnasco The Tame Raven

Bazzani Christ in the Garden of Olives

Canaletto The Grand Canal, Venice

Bellotto Landscape

Tiepolo Erection of the Statue to an Emperor

Guardi Landscape with a Canal

Guardi Arch and Shore

FLEMISH SCHOOL

Hans Memling St Benedict

Hans Memling Portrait of a Man

Hans Memling Portrait of a Man

Gerard David
The Adoration of the Magi

Hans Memling
Portrait of Benedetto di Tommaso Portinari

Civetta The Copper Mines

Pieter Breugel Orpheus in the Underworld

Van Dyck
Portraits of Charles I of England and Henrietta of France

Van Dyck
Portrait of Jean de Montfort

Frans Pourbus
Portrait of a young Prince

Frans Pourbus
Portrait of a young Princess

Frans Pourbus
Eleonora of Mantua as a Child

Rubens
Portrait of Isabella Brandt

Rubens The Three Graces

Rubens Ulysses on the Island of the Phaeacians

Sustermans Portrait of Ferdinand II

Sustermans Portrait of a Child

Sustermans Portrait of a Woman

Sustermans Portrait of Galileo

Sustermans Portrait of Prince Waldemar
Christian of Denmark

GERMAN SCHOOL

Dürer The Apostle St Philip

Dürer The Madonna and Child

Dürer The Apostle St James

Dürer Portrait of the Artist's Father

Altdorfer The Martyrdom of St Florian

Cranach St George

Cranach Self-Portrait

Cranach
Portraits of Luther and his Wife

Cranach
Johann I and Friedrich III, Electors of Saxony

SPANISH SCHOOL

Luis de Morales Christ bearing the Cross

Ribera St Francis

DUTCH SCHOOL

Master of the Virgo inter Virgines
The Crucifixion

Joos van Cleeve
Portrait of a Man

Joos van Cleeve
Portrait of a Woman

Antonio Moro Self-Portrait

Gabriel Metsu
The Hunter and the Lady

Jan Lys The Sacrifice of Isaac

Jan Lys The Prodigal Son

Van Mieris The Charlatan

Van Aelst Dead Birds

Jan Steen The Luncheon

Van Ruysch Flowers, Fruit and Insects

Van Ruysch Flowers and Fruit

Van Ruysch Flowers and Fruit

Van Poelenburg Landscape with Ruins and Peasants

FRENCH SCHOOL

Nicolas Froment
Martha and Magdalen at the Feet of Christ

Nicolas Froment
Donors of the Triptych and the Madonna and Child

Mignard Portrait of
Françoise-Marguerite de Grignan

Rigaud Portrait of Bossuet

Largilliere Portrait of Rousseau

Nattier Portrait of Marie-Zéphyrine, niece of Louis XV

Chardin A Boy playing Cards

LIST OF ILLUSTRATIONS

Numbers in bold type denote colour plates

INDEX OF NAMES

Numbers in italics refer to illustrations